A Miscellany of Puzzles:
Mathematical and Otherwise

By the Author

Experiments in Topology

A Miscellany of Puzzles:
Mathematical and Otherwise

STEPHEN BARR

A Miscellany of Puzzles

Mathematical and Otherwise

ILLUSTRATED

THOMAS Y. CROWELL COMPANY

NEW YORK

My thanks to Dr. Rex Depew, Charles W. Trigg, Ronald M. Foster, and Milton Boyd for help in preparing the manuscript. And to the following for allowing me to reprint some of my puzzles which first appeared in their publications: Martin Gardner of *Scientific American*, A. C. Spectorsky of *Playboy Magazine*, Joseph Madachy of *Recreational Mathematics Magazine*, and to Margaret Farrar of *The New York Times* for permission to use a version of my crossword puzzle that appeared there.

Designed by Albert Burkhardt.
Illustrated by Arnold Dobrin.
Manufactured in the United States of America
by the Vail-Ballou Press, Inc., Binghamton, New York.
Library of Congress Catalog Card No. 65-14905
1 2 3 4 5 6 7 8 9 10

From an address by Dr. Sylvan Moore,

given at the Regent's Club in London, 1954

A puzzle, as opposed to a problem, is presumably something you take pleasure in solving, otherwise why are you solving it? I don't think the answer should be so surprising as to challenge credibility, but I think it's all right if one says, "Dammit, why didn't I think of that?"

A real-life puzzle, like the ones we were discussing just now before we got on math, where you are looking for a murderer, may depend on the discovery of some arcane fact—the sort that Sherlock Holmes collected—but the answer to a regular puzzle should not involve some piece of information that is not generally known, nor susceptible to being worked out.

A puzzle may be pawky, even a little underhanded, but in that case the answer must have its own kind of authenticity. I once asked my youngest grandchild, who I thought had started geometry—I am a very poor judge of ages—if she knew how to make a square. She said, "Yes. You cut off the corners of a circle."

Contents

1

Two Glasses of Port

A and B have 16 ounces of port and two 8-ounce glasses, which they fill. Their schnauzer likes port, too —it's not good for him—and drinks 5 ounces from B's glass. But in the meanwhile B has by mistake drunk 3 ounces out of A's glass. The glasses have graduation marks and the men's initials. The men like to drink out of their own glasses, and they are both fair-minded and a little muddleheaded.

"Here," A says, "it's not fair for you to bear *all* the loss of the 5 ounces the dog took: I'll give you enough of mine to make the glasses level." But B shakes his head.

"I agree we should share the 5-ounce loss, but don't forget I drank 3 ounces of *your* port. See, I'm returning it." It is, in fact, all that's left in his glass, and it fills A's glass to the top again. "Now we'll share what the dog left us." A pours half the glass into B's.

"Well," says A, "it comes out the same as my scheme: half a glass each, so we must have got it right."

Had they? If not, what should now be done to correct things? (Try it without paper and pencil.)

Answer on page 109

2

The Web on the Doll's House

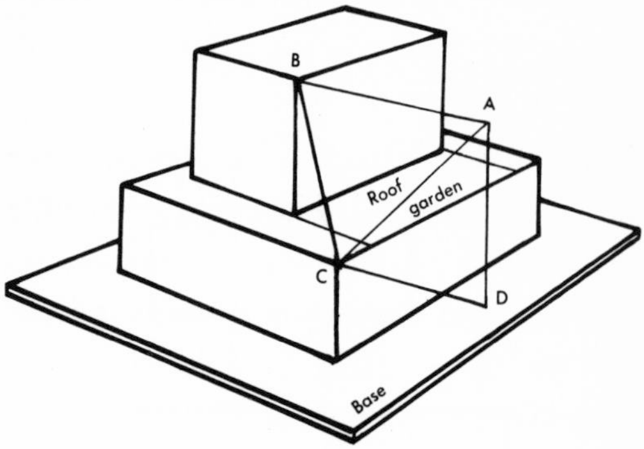

The illustration shows a modernistic doll's house on a flat base, and AD, a vertical flagpole standing before the center of its symmetrical front. On the setback is a rectangular roof garden, measuring one by two units. The flagpole is two units high. All surfaces are rectangles.

During the night a mathematical, but otherwise harmless, spider has strung webs, connecting A, B, C and D, as shown by the thin lines. He observes the odd fact that all four of them are the same length as the flagpole, and he is toying with the idea of putting in a fifth web, from B to D.

If he did, how long would it be in terms of the doll's house or any part thereof?

Answer on page 74

3

A Patriarchal Cross

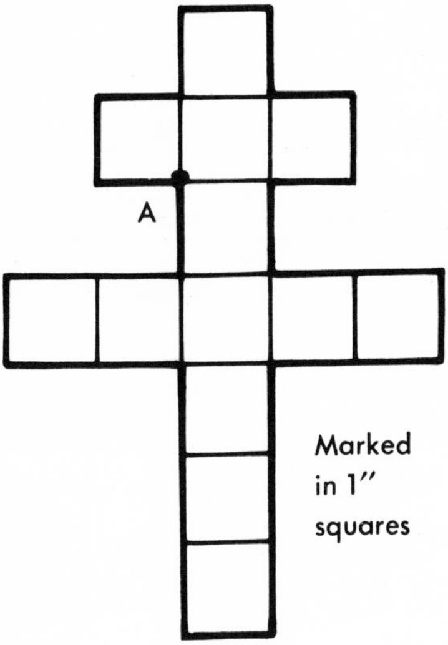

With one continuous straight cut touching point A, divide this Patriarchal Cross into two pieces of equal area. The proof must be in elementary geometry, and involve only rational proportions—i.e., rational fractions. Only ruler and compass allowed.

Answer on page 76

4

Concealing the Edge

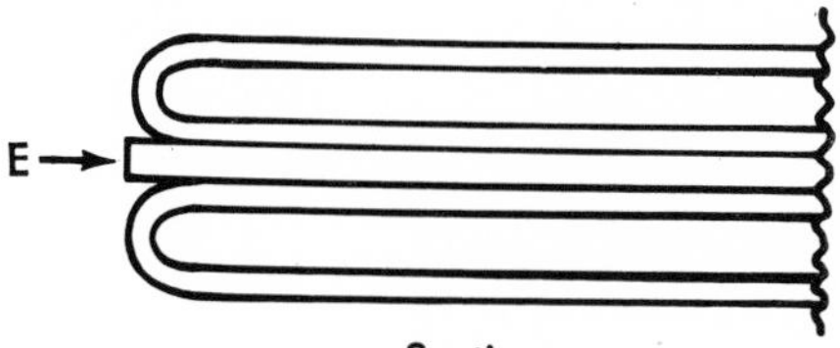

Section

You have a 5-inch square of paper which has a red border on both sides having a width of ⅛ inch. The actual edge of the paper is also colored red. It is required to fold the paper so that all the red is hidden. This means that any part of an edge—even a corner—is regarded as not hidden if flush with the covering parts, as in magnified section shown here: E must be recessed at least ⅛ inch. If the paper has been folded, and a new fold consequently makes more than one crease, the new fold is nonetheless regarded as *one.*

What is the minimum number of folds?

Answer on page 78

5

Cube Formation

You have a paper rectangle measuring 1 by 3 units. Cut it (using straight line cuts) into two identical pieces which can be folded and joined to make a cube. No overlaps or gaps allowed. Use the minimum number of cuts.

Answer on page 80

6

The Man in the Bucket

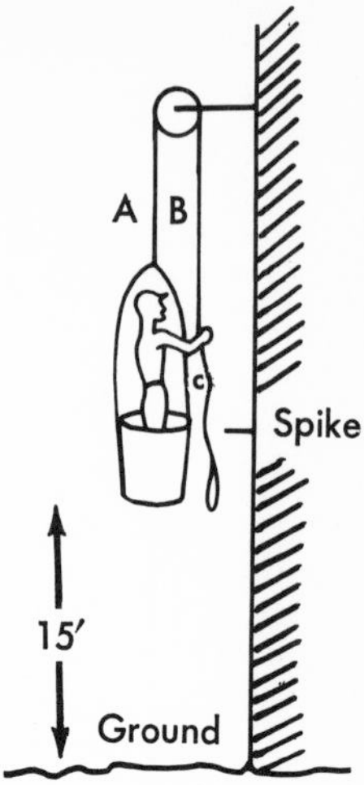

A man is standing in a bucket that is attached to the end of a rope, A, which goes over a pulley, and he holds the other part, B. In front of him is a wall. The part of the rope, C, that is below his hand is 5 feet long, and has a loop on its end. He wants his lunch. He is tired of holding that rope. He lets himself down until he is holding the loop, which he slips over a convenient spike in the wall. The whole rope is 25 feet long and is slightly elastic, so that at the first stage (shown here) the A and B part of the rope is stretched to its maximum extent—and to within 90% of breaking point—and he is 15 feet from the ground. The rope stretches one inch per foot. How far is he from the ground after he hooks the rope over the spike? (Ignore loop.) Give answer to nearest half inch.

Answer on page 79

7

How Many Pieces?

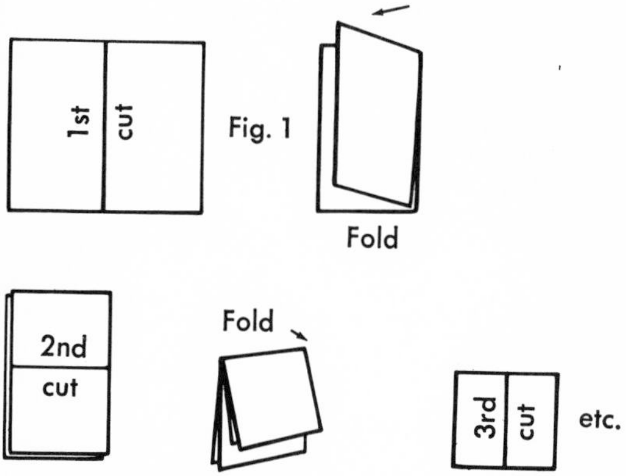

Fig. 1 Fig. 2 Fig. 3

Take a square of paper and cut almost across (as in Fig. 1). Then fold as shown and cut again almost across (Fig. 2). Now fold at right angles to the previous fold and cut again as before (Fig. 3). Continue doing this, but at the sixth cut keep on all the way across. How many separate pieces will you have?

What is the expression showing the final number of pieces for any number of cuts (not including the last complete one)? Try to answer the first question in your head. Then try making a sort of diagram to show what happens. (Experiments with more than about eight folds are out—you can't fold that many.)

Answer on page 121

8

Slow—Therefore Early

A man is given reliable information about the time of arrival of something at a place X. On this he bases an estimate of its arrival at another place, Y. He makes his own guess as to its speed (which is constant), but he is wrong. Otherwise his information—as to the position of X and Y and time of arrival at X—is correct. The something arrives at Y *sooner* than he estimates, and because the something traveled *slower* than he thought. Explain, and give a real-life example.

Answer on page 127

9

Wolf in Sheep's Compound

A wolf is crossing a wasteland and arrives in a starving condition halfway across, and too weak to go farther, when he finds an enclosure of iron bars completely surrounding some fat sheep—too fat to get through the bars, natch. The wolf is so thin he can but he knows he will be too fat to get out if he eats enough sheep-flesh to keep him going to cross the wasteland. The fence is too high to jump and unbreakable. The shepherd will be coming the next week with a gun, and the wolf cannot undergo another starvation period like the last. What is his best strategy?

Answer on page 75

10

Mutually Faster

There are two animals, A and B, on an unlimited and unobstructed plain. If A wants to catch B and B wants to escape A, and B has a 20-yard start: A can *always* catch B. But if B wants to catch A, and A wants to escape B, and A has a 20-yard start, B can *always* catch A. How come, and what animals can they be?

Answer on page 79

11

Two Rhymes of Age

These verses are the general equations that lie behind the old riddle of *How Old is Anne?* (Women, children, and lawyers seem to be able to do the first in their heads, but mathematicians absolutely have to be allowed to have paper and pencil.)

1 Pray the ratio of ages infer,
(Use of pencil and paper I bar),
If I'm twice as old as you were
When I was as old as you are.

2 The proof of this please let your mind engage:
No matter how much older you may be
Than I was when you were my present age,
You can't be more than twice as old as me.

Answers on page 107

12

The Seven Animals

There are seven animals (and no others): a lion, a hyena, a poodle and her puppy, a Siamese cat and her kitten and a Great Dane. They all belong to either one of only two suborders. One of the animals is called X and one of them—a different one—is called Y.

The pupils of the lion's eyes have a different shape from the pupils of X's eyes.

The hyena is a member of the same suborder as Y.

Y has never touched X.

Which animal is Y?

The answer must be unique—without alternatives.

Answer on page 100

13

The String and the Salt Shaker

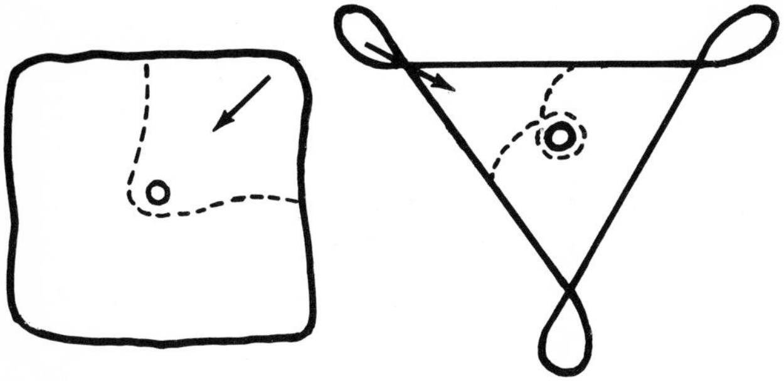

You have a single loop of string which you put on the floor in a rough square, with a salt shaker in the middle. You then bring a corner of the square loop over the shaker, as shown here by the dotted line. If you do this with all four corners, how many circuits of string will be around the shaker?

If you make a triangle and then twist each apex clockwise, and bring the resultant loops over the shaker, how many circuits of string will there be around the shaker? Both questions must be answered without using string or pencil and paper.

Answers on page 82

14

Spills

In making a spill—a twisted strip of paper used for getting a light from a fire—we have torn a strip from a newspaper, so that one edge is smooth and one ragged. We can start the rolling at either of the two corners:

Supposing we want the ragged edge concealed, which method should we use? In fact, without using paper, which of the above will give which of these results?

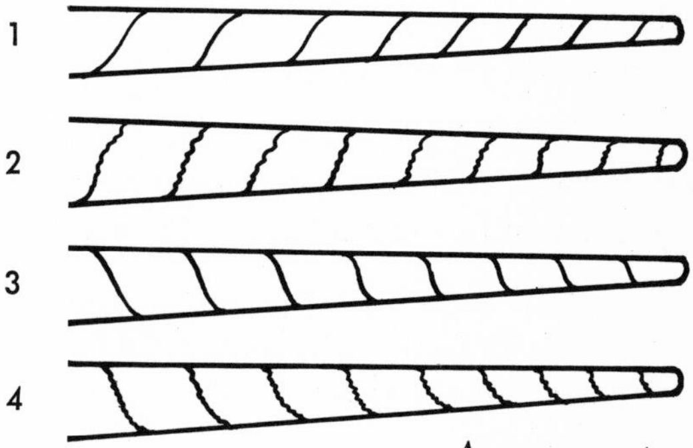

Answers on page 84

15

The Vacant Lot

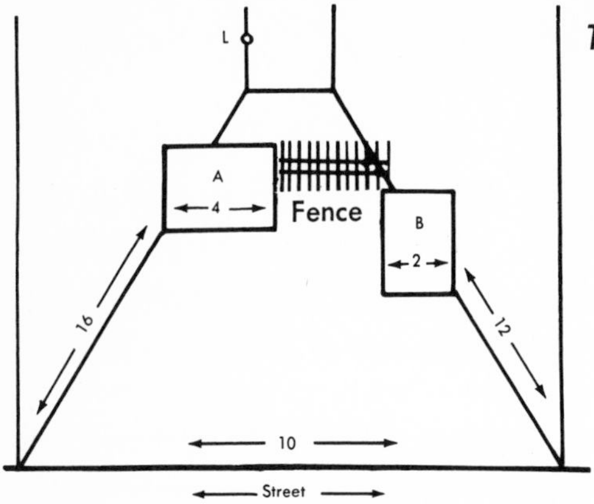

In this vacant lot, 10 yards wide, are two sections of wall sticking out from the parallel sides. At the far corner is a lamp L, which can be seen by Pete as he comes home from school along the street in the evening. He has trespassed as far as the fence, and paced out the dimensions shown in yards. The owner builds two rectangular sheds (everything in the lot is rectangular) one in front of B and one behind A, using A and B as end walls. He tells Pete that the two sheds are in the same proportions of length to width, but not how big they are. He also puts up a new fence along the street. Pete finds he can still just get a glimpse of the lamp between the *far* corner of shed A and the *near* corner of shed B. No longer able to measure anything, he can nonetheless calculate the depth of the lot. What is it?

Answer on page 77

16

Paper Stars

As everyone knows, stars can be made by folding and cutting paper. A star will be defined as a regular figure with acute points: a pentagon wouldn't do, as the apexes are obtuse, but Fig. 1 is a 5-pointed star. It is actually a decagon with alternate angles re-entrant. In this puzzle we are restricted to one straight cut, but varying numbers of folds.

Fig. 1

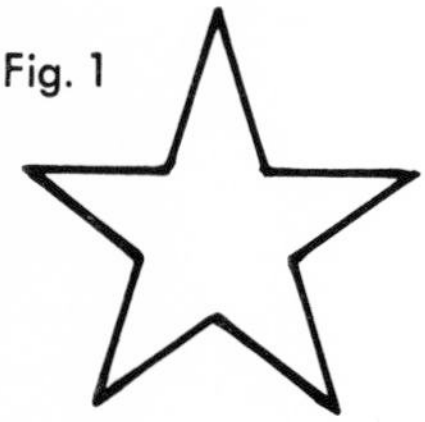

Fig. 2

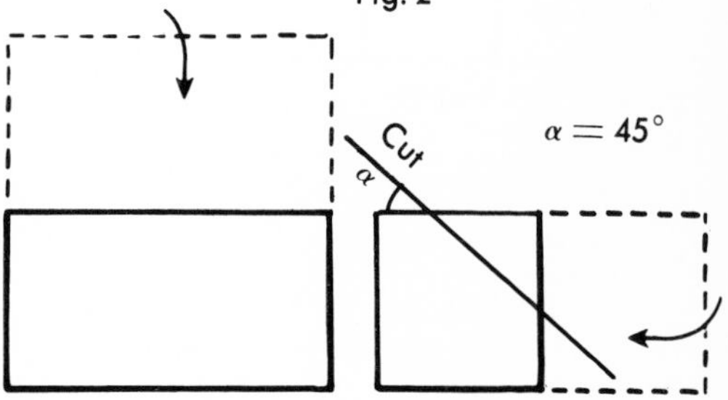

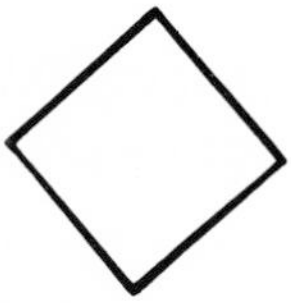

Fig. 3

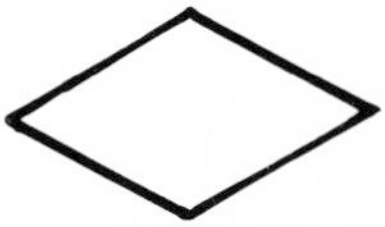

Fig. 4

With one fold we cannot make anything, but with two folds (Fig. 2) we can make a square, Fig. 3, which is not a star, since the corners are not acute. However, we can make a 2-pointed "star" if we tilt the cut either way from 45° (Fig. 4). With three folds (Fig. 5) we get a real 4-pointed star, Fig. 6, and by altering the folds (Fig. 7), a 3-pointed star, Fig. 8.

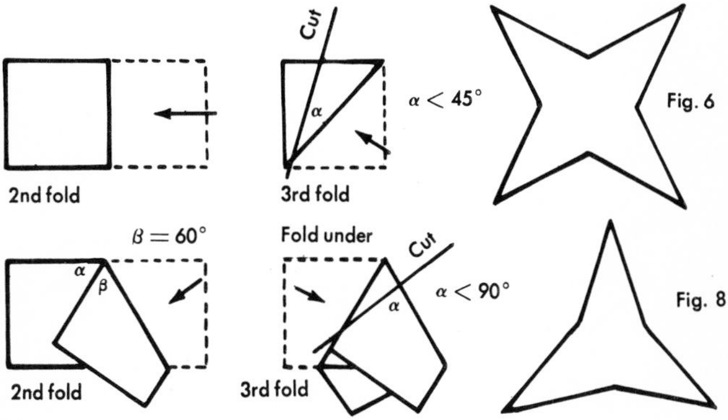

Fig. 5 (1st fold as before)

Fig. 6

Fig. 7 (1st fold as before)

Fig. 8

Problem A: With four folds make a 5-pointed and a 6-pointed star. (We can get 8 points with one more diagonal fold in Fig. 5.)

Problem B: Make a 3-pointed star with an *even* number of folds.

Answers on pages 81 and 82

17

The Moebius Hat Trick

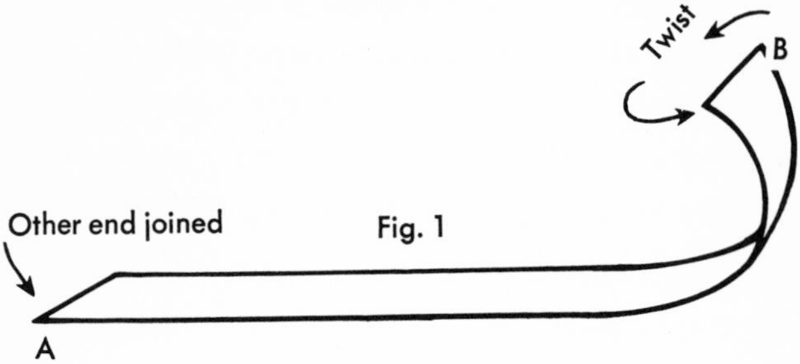

Fig. 1

Fig. 2

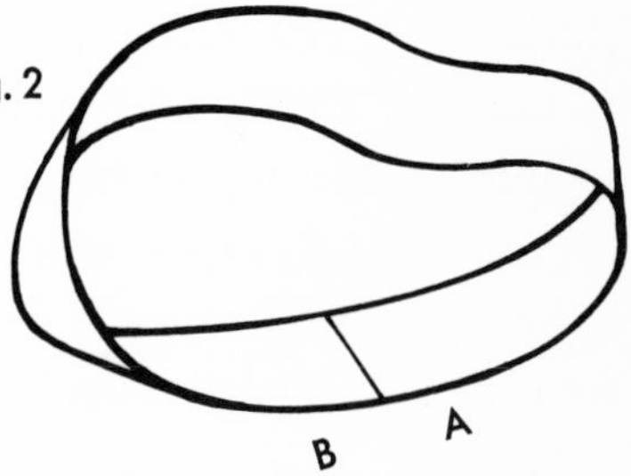

A Moebius strip is a parallel strip of paper that is given a half twist, Fig. 1, and joined end to end, Fig. 2. Since this has the effect of joining the front to the back, and edge A to edge B, it has only one side and one edge. Various oddities result: when a line is drawn lengthwise down the center it eventually runs on both "sides," and when we cut along this line, the strip remains in one piece. To do these puzzles, pencil, paper, and scissors are needed.

If we use rather springy paper, like a good grade of heavy bond, 1 by 10 inches, the loop makes an irregular flattened oval, Fig. 2. Pulling out the sides only makes it triangular. But the original strip does not have to be rectangular: for the sake of this puzzle we shall merely require it to be parallel, like a road, if curved.

Puzzle 1: By experiment and analysis find the best shape of strip which gives a nearly circular hole when formed into a Moebius strip.

Puzzle 2: The above is the preliminary to the main point: Can a Moebius strip be used as the brim of a hat? This boils down to attaching the edge, or rather, *part* of the edge to a cylinder—the crown of a hat is cylindrical where it surrounds the head. It will be evident on inspection that no matter how we distort or cut the end of a hollow cylinder, it cannot be made to join all of the edge of a Moebius strip, as the edge crosses over itself. Just make a reasonable-looking hat —pretty, if possible.

Answers on page 86

18

The Pool and the Patriot

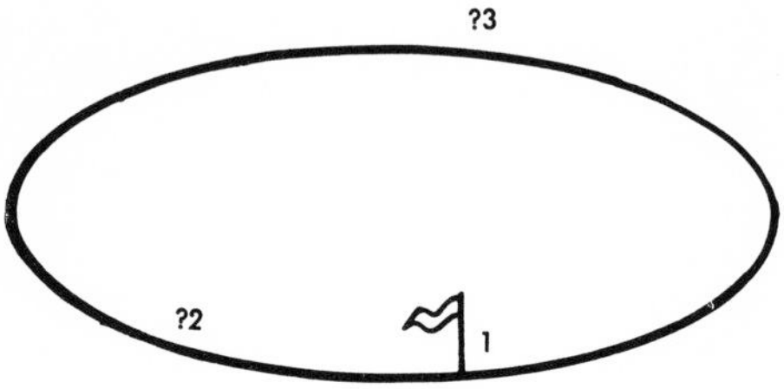

A man had a circular pool, 100 feet across, and two flags, which he decided to place on its edge so that the shorter distance between them—measured around the edge—had the same ratio to the longer distance as the longer distance had to the whole circumference. As he placed the first flag a friend arrived with a third flag. (He was a mathematician.)

"Now," said this man, "you will have to arrange things so that the first space is to the second as the second is to the first and second combined; *and* the second space will be to the third as the third is to the second and third combined, I'm afraid."

"Oh, dear," said the owner, "where will Flag 3 go?"

"I can't give you its exact distance from Flag 2 offhand," said the friend, "but I can tell you how far it'll be from Flag 1, measured *across* the pool in a bee line."

Why was this easier, and what is the distance?

Answer on page 83

19

Anagrams

The classic anagram has the same number of words as its original, but the famous one of Florence Nightingale, *Flit on, Cheering Angel,* is so apposite that we don't care. The only excuse for an anagram is that it is apposite or timely. When it is neither, the excuse must be manufactured. In the following the anagrams are italicized.

1 He bought the house sight-unseen; it collapsed, and he found a sign on it: *Vacate Pro Tem.* (two words)
2 He *Noticed* that his comb was on edge. (one word)
3 "Watch the *Cuckoo-Twirl Scene!*" he sneered. (one word)

Answers on page 84

20

The Infinite Chessboard

Fig. 1

Fig. 2

64 sq. 12 or 13

Fig. 3

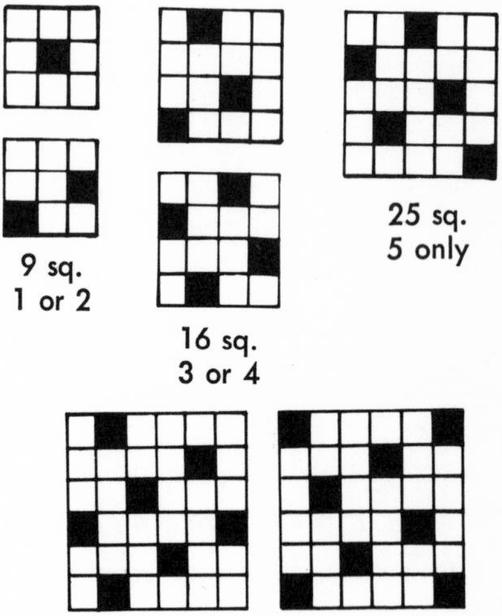

9 sq. 1 or 2

16 sq. 3 or 4

25 sq. 5 only

36 sq. 7 or 8

On the 8-by-8 board in Fig. 1, the black squares are so placed that each is a chess knight's move away from its neighbors. If we shift them all one square to the left, we can get thirteen black squares instead of twelve into the board, as in Fig. 2. The smaller diagrams in Fig. 3 give the numbers that can be fitted this way into boards containing 9, 16, 25 and 36 squares. It will be seen that the numbers of black squares increase in a somewhat irregular way. The question is: What would the proportion be of black to white squares if this pattern were continued on an infinitely big board?

Answer on page 118

21

Rubber Bands

Fig. 1

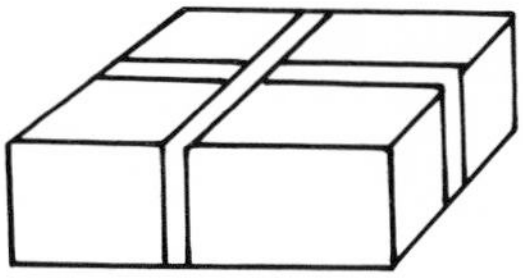

Fig. 2

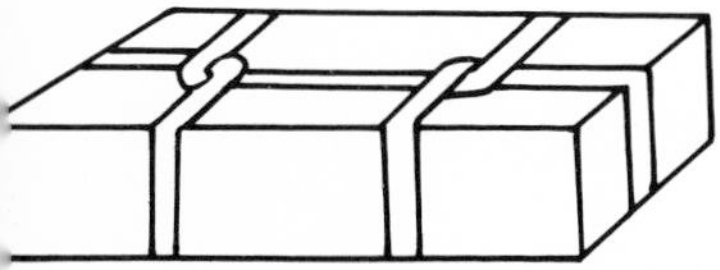

Fig. 3

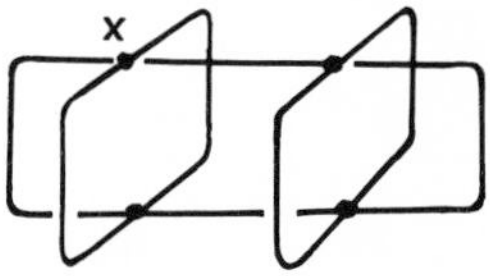

Fig. 4

It is possible to tie a box with one piece of ribbon so that there are no twists, if we regard the manner in which the ribbon is looped around itself in Fig. 1 as being not twisted. Thus the ribbon could be looped as in Figs. 2 and 3, for example (we ignore the knot), but would it be possible to arrange a rubber band in these two ways? The difference would be in the fact that the band is already joined in an untwisted loop. All that is required is that the band follow the general pattern, as shown diagrammatically in Fig. 4, and the four junctions like *x* can be direct crossings as in Fig. 2, or linkings as in Fig. 3. (*Continued*)

21 *Continued*

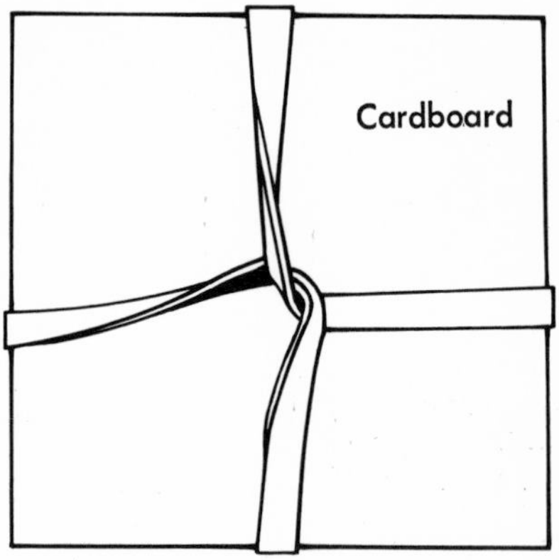

Fig. 5

For the experiment use a large, flat rubber band, at least 3 inches long unstretched, and a stiff cardboard rectangle about 1½ by 2 inches. The linking of the Fig. 1 kind will look like Fig. 5, and we see that in the sense of what was said, the band is not actually twisted: the top surface remains on top.

So that the reader will not waste time, the arrangements of Figs. 2 and 5 cannot be made without twists. But Fig. 4 can. How?

Answer on page 93

22

Irregular Growth

A man notices that an unusual, but inconvenient, eyelash is growing at such an angle that it tickles his eye. He plucks it out with tweezers. Then it happens again . . . and again. Finally he realizes that the occurrence is at highly irregular intervals, and he decides to keep track. Four days had intervened between the previous two hair-pullings, but this time it was 12 days. Then 12 again, then—to his surprise—4. Then a long pause—16 days—then 4, then 12 and then again 12.

"Ha!" he said, "I know what's happening, and I know when the next will be!" When will it be, and why?

Answer on page 92

23

The Ingenious Restorer

A restorer of paintings was asked to fix a badly spotted mural. The owner said, "There are mildew spots all over it, mostly tiny, and I want them left as they give it an antique look, but will you paint out the 10 or 15 biggest ones on the sky—they look like bugs or something." The restorer went to work and did as requested, but the owner came back and said, "I see you haven't painted out the biggest ones yet."

Sure enough, the next 10 or 15 biggest ones now stood out, so the restorer offered to paint out all of them by redoing the sky, but the owner said it wouldn't go with the rest of the mural, and he couldn't afford to have it all done over. So the restorer tried again, with the same result: the *next* 10 or 15 biggest ones stood out and looked like bugs or something.

Question: The spots graded down in size to myriads of microscopic dots, so one couldn't count how many there were. The restorer realized that, no matter how far he carried on the process, there would always be the next 10 or 15 biggest: what did he do?

Answer on page 107

24

Cryptarithmetic

An Alphametic, or Cryptarithm, is a sum in arithmetic that is written down, but with letters substituted for the numbers, like a simple cipher. The puzzle then is to work out what numbers the various letters stand for. The simplest example might be the following, of which we are told that it is a multiplication of the first digit by the second, with the result written underneath the line, (and that A is positive):

```
A
A
—
A
```

Since the same letter always stands for the same number, the answer must be A = 1, because 1 is the only number that fills the bill.

Sometimes symbols instead of letters are used, as in the following, where the dots stand for *any* number, and not necessarily the same one. Which particular operation is which, is given at the side, and there is only one possible answer. (The "1," of course, means 1.)

```
      . .
      . .   (multiply)
    -----
    . . .
  . . .
  -------
  . . . .
    1 . .   (add)
---------
. . . . .
```

Answer on page 85

25

Man and Belt

Fig. 1

Fig. 2

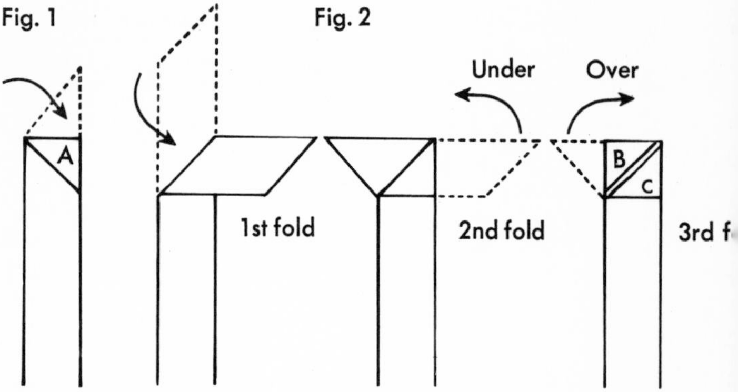

A man had a bathrobe with a belt which he always rolled up when traveling. One end was cut off at an angle of 45°, and it annoyed him that there was an irregularity of thickness because of this. So he tried folding it in various ways to make the end rectangular.

Merely folding down the tip wouldn't do, Fig. 1, as the double thickness at A would not be rectangular. The method in Fig. 2 made the end square and the extra thickness rectangular, but there were two layers at B and three at C. Subsequent maneuvering failed to correct the fault. How did he finally do it?

Answer on page 112

26

Morse Code

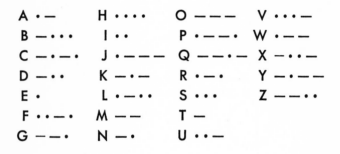

A •—	H ••••	O ———	V •••—
B —•••	I ••	P •——•	W •——
C —•—•	J •———	Q ——•—	X —••—
D —••	K —•—	R •—•	Y —•——
E •	L •—••	S •••	Z ——••
F ••—•	M ——	T —	
G ——•	N —•	U ••—	

This is the International Morse Code. Learning it is a nuisance, and since sending is easier to learn than receiving, the latter is the best one to start with. For the sender, the list given above is the logical one. Since it is in alphabetical order, it is easy to find the letter we want, and next to it the symbol. But, in the case of receiving, what is the most logical—and most easily used—arrangement in which to put the *symbols,* if we want to look for a symbol we have just heard, and there is no time to waste? (Ignore punctuation, numerals, etc.)

Answer on page 94

27

The Half-Hidden Balance

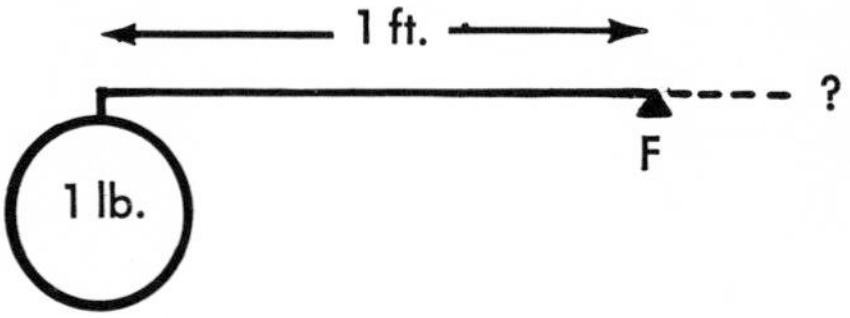

The horizontal line is a weightless rod, balanced on fulcrum at F, and of unknown length to the right of the fulcrum. The visible part is 1 foot long, and supports a 1-pound weight. Besides being weightless, the rod is able to support any weight and, since it is in balance, there must be a weight to the right. The further the second weight is to the right, the less it can be. What are the lower and upper limits of the total possible force downward at F?

Answer on page 85

28

Stellated Tetrahedron

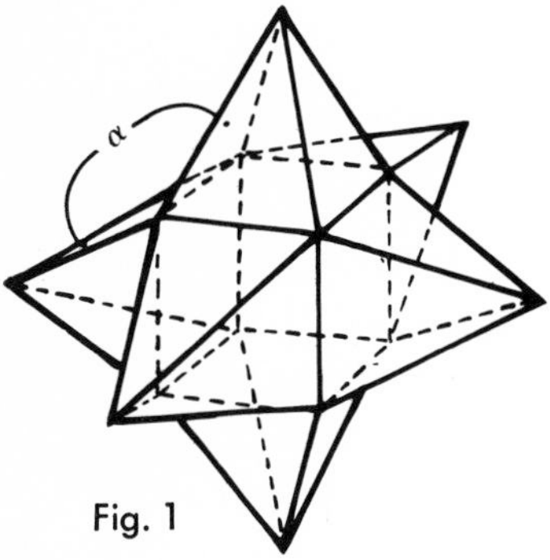

Fig. 1

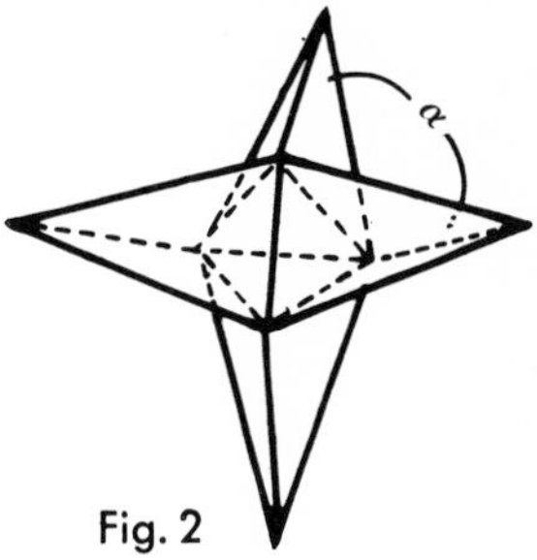

Fig. 2

A *stellated* regular polyhedron is one with (equal) pyramids constructed on the original faces. Fig. 1 shows a stellated cube: it has 24 faces instead of six. It will be noticed that there are two faces for every edge of the original cube: a general rule. Also the dihedral angles like α are re-entrant. Nothing has been said about the altitudes of the pyramids except that they are equal. If we take a stellated tetrahedron—a Rhododendrahedron?—Fig. 2, and begin to reduce the altitude of its pyramids, the dihedral angles like α will obviously increase. At some point they will become 180°. How is the resultant polyhedron described in ordinary English?

Answer on page 95

29

Tetrahedron in Cube

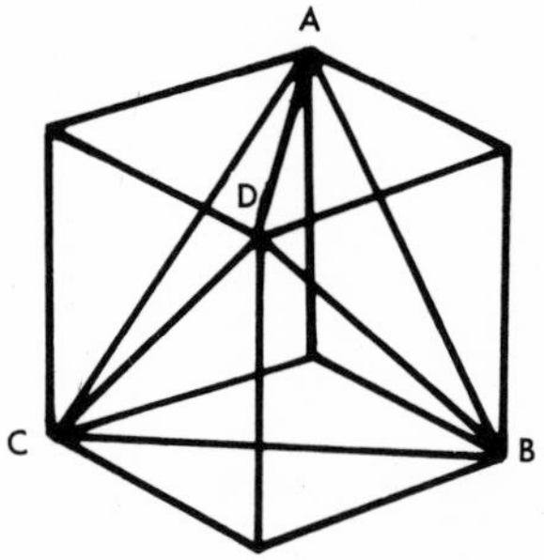

The figure shows the biggest tetrahedron that is contained in a cube. The cube measures 1 unit on the edge, so the tetrahedron is therefore $\sqrt{2}$ on the edge. Without pencil and paper or adding to the diagram, give the volume of the tetrahedron, ABCD. This means that the proof must be given in the form of simple geometric statements or equations.

Answer on page 113

30

Section of the Square

With straight cuts, cut a square piece of paper into 20 identical pieces. Being paper, they may be turned over, so some may be mirror images of the others, but no cut may be parallel to an edge of the square—otherwise we could cut it into any number of identical parallel strips.

Answer on page 97

31

The Unreliable Appliance

What nontechnical appliance found in most houses will, when something goes wrong, describe an exact elliptical path? The proviso is made that no wall or other vertical surfaces are touched or involved. Theoretically the path is precise; in practice and under the right circumstances it will be very nearly so. State the circumstances and which part of the appliance will describe the elliptical path.

Answer on page 108

32

A Photograph in Winter

A rural wood; the sky is grey,
The trees are bare except for one:
A hemlock, higher than the rest,
And evergreen, it caught the snow.
Its upper branches hold the most.
The lower parts are naked now.
What can we tell about the wind,
If any blew, since the snow fell?

Answer on page 96

33

Visualizing Puzzles

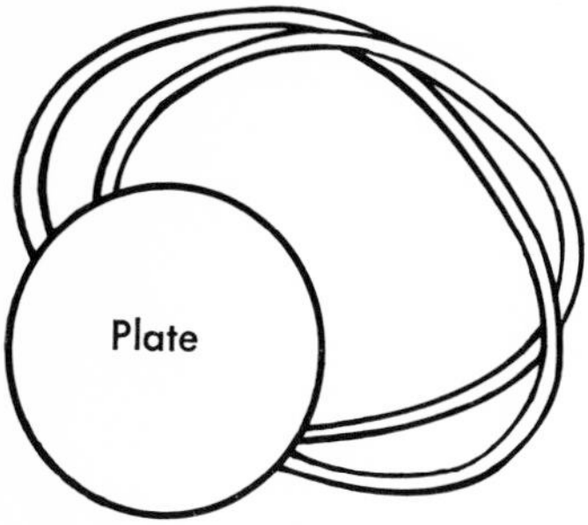

Fig. 1

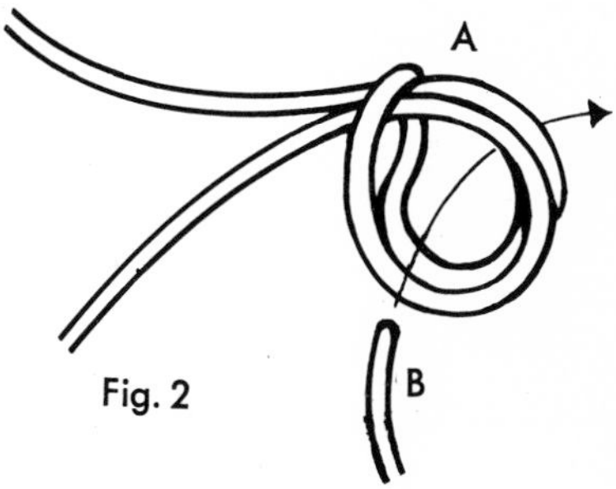

Fig. 2

Fig. 1 shows a continuous loop of cord—one without ends—partly concealed by a plate. Mr. A has seen *only* the part now hidden, and cannot tell us whether the loop has a knot in it: Mr. B has seen the *whole* loop, and reports that it has a single, simple knot in it. Draw what is under the plate.

In Fig. 2 the two cords—not loops since they each have two ends—are as shown, and B is passed through A as shown by the arrow. When everything is pulled taut, what kind of knot results? Answer this without actually using any string.

Answers on page 99

34

97%

This is to be solved in the head, without paper and pencil. Time limit 10 seconds. If some coffee is "97% caffeine-free," how many cups of it would one have to drink to get the amount of caffeine in a cup of regular coffee?

Answer on page 127

35

The Man in the Milk Carton

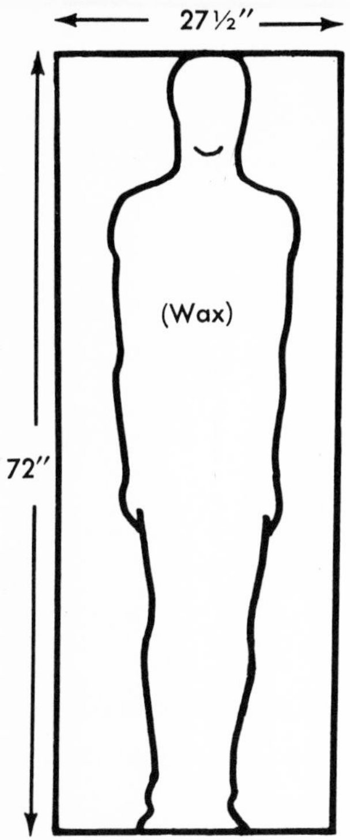

A full-size wax replica of a six-foot, 160-pound man is in a box that happens to have the same shape and proportions as an ordinary milk carton. Being of wax, it can be melted down. Estimate, within 10% or better, how many more wax men like him can be melted down and poured with him into the box. (Try to do it without a tape measure; using only common knowledge: e.g., a milk carton is 7¼ inches high.*)

Answer on page 117

* Not so commonly known, perhaps—except to dairymen.

36

Five Squares into One

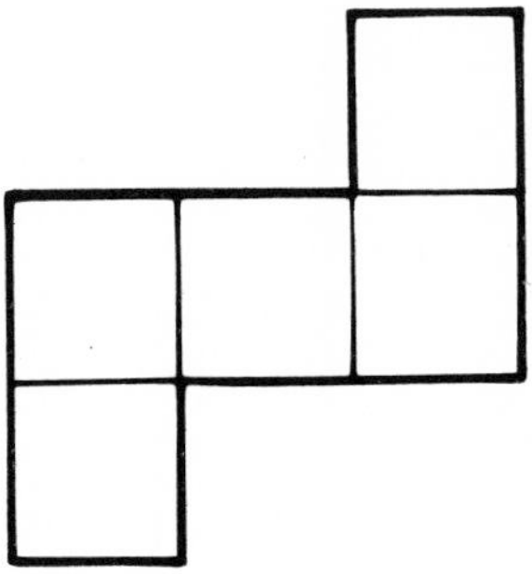

The figure shown is to be cut and reformed into a square. It is composed of five squares, but it is now in one piece. The problem is to do it by cutting it into *three pieces*, and with only two straight cuts. The pieces may not be rearranged after the first cut, but left in their original position. (The German mathematician, Hilbert, proved that any polygon can be transformed into any other of equal area, and in a finite number of cuts and pieces, but the number may be very large. Here it must be two cuts and three pieces.)

Answer on page 104

37

In Your Head

It is required that this puzzle be done in the head; proof being given in the form of simple geometrical and arithmetical statements, and without diagrams. It would be merely laborious to do it otherwise—just a problem in a geometry book.

The dual of a polyhedron is another polyhedron whose vertices are at the centroids of the faces of the first polyhedron. A centroid is a kind of geometric center, corresponding to the center of gravity; so that the centroid of a square is the point where its diagonals intersect. The centroid of a triangle is the point of intersection of the three medians: lines joining the vertices with the mid-points of the opposite sides.

The question is: What is the volume of the dual of a regular tetrahedron with a volume of one?

Answer on page 119

38

Handicapping Puzzle

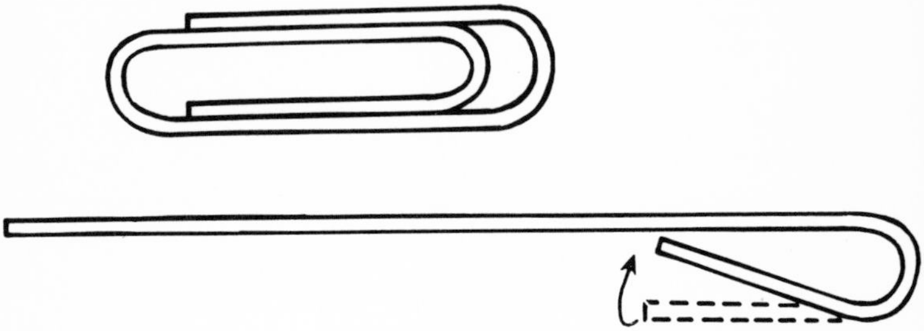

Fig. 1

This is a problem in handicapping. Take a paper clip, open it out straight except for the smaller crook, and bend the latter together as in Fig. 1. Break off a short piece from the wide, flat end of a toothpick, and hang the clip on it as shown, but do not make any of the movements described until specified. If the piece of wood is held edge-up by thumb and forefinger on either side of the clip, the clip can be given a sharp flick with one of the other fingers, so that it will spin around, finally losing momentum and coming to rest. The number of rotations will depend upon how hard it is flicked, and, if the original impulse is just right, the clip could stop rotating when at the top of its turn.

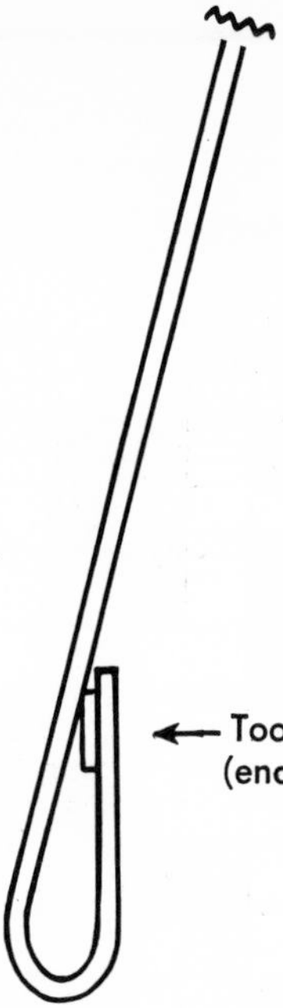

Fig. 2

Now make the following experiment: Hold the piece of wood as shown, but with one hand, and with the other hold the clip upright and let it go. It will drop and catch, Fig. 2, so that it remains stuck in this position. Then try this at various angles to find the approximate angular limits within which this will happen. *Do not spin the clip:* assuming the person who does the flicking has not been practicing, and from what can now be surmised, estimate the chances of this sticking upright happening three times in succession, in any three tries.

Answer on page 105

39

Two-in-One Crossword Puzzle

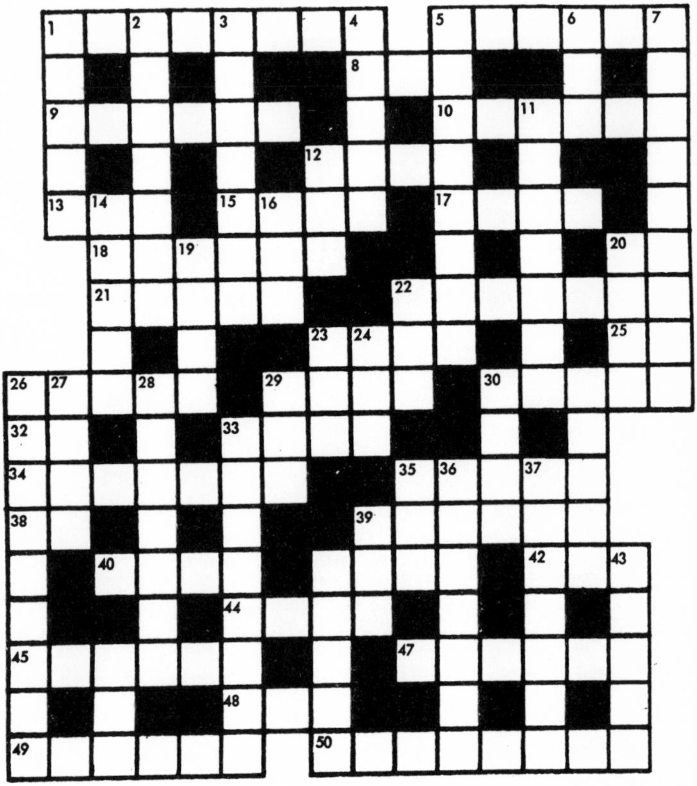

This puzzle combines some of the features of the English kind—i.e., many unkeyed letters—with the more or less straightforward definitions of the American, or regular kind. There are no anagrams. Although we do not lean over backwards to be fair to the solver, all the words are well known, and the definitions guaranteed to be correct and to be found in abridged dictionaries.

Across

1 Useful foreign invention (ends in Z)
5 Describing something determined by the planets
8 Little troublemaker
9 Elevated
10 Notre Dame — Penn State
12 Classical lover in a rather ostensible way
13 Military group (abbr.)
15 Joe Louis beat him
17 What 15 might do to his opponent
18 Plan of the Colosseum, e.g.
20 Book of O.T.
21 One of three
22 A novice might be this
23 What dissidents are likely to do
25 Musical note
26 Descriptive of some complexions
29 Mark Twain spoke of him as "experienced, industrious, ambitious and quite often picturesque"
30 Religious dignitary (sounds as if he came earlier)
32 A measurement (abbr.)
33 Ice in a certain form
34 Two-wheeled job
35 That which limits
38 An element (abbr.)
39 Cleo's chap
40 Something round
41 Bearded one
42 Something objected to by the Amer. colonists
44 A London park
45 Close, as a look
47 Part of ancient Greece
48 Bird
49 Caught, as a fish
50 Spiked plants

39 *Continued*

Down

1 Harsh, as some wine
2 Many hope to see this at a gallery
3 Lab apparatus
4 Mr. Stripes
5 Word for what comes directly from something
6 Something that sticks out radially
7 Female parliamentarian
11 Separate
12 Some claim she came first
14 Hemmed
16 Word associated with Methuselah
19 Red jewel
20 Linguistic comb. form
22 Musical abbr.
23 By
24 This is important aboard
26 One word for the Irish Troubles
27 Head, or tooth
28 What Monday is as opposed to Monday night
29 Payment of a kind
30 Pope, c.150 AD
31 Oriental god
33 Like an ancient tree
35 Legal abbr.
36 Royalty at ancient Thebes
37 Wild
39 White House nickname
41 Decorate
43 Roentgen emanations
46 Make stitches a certain way

Answer on page 120

40

Strictly Geometrical

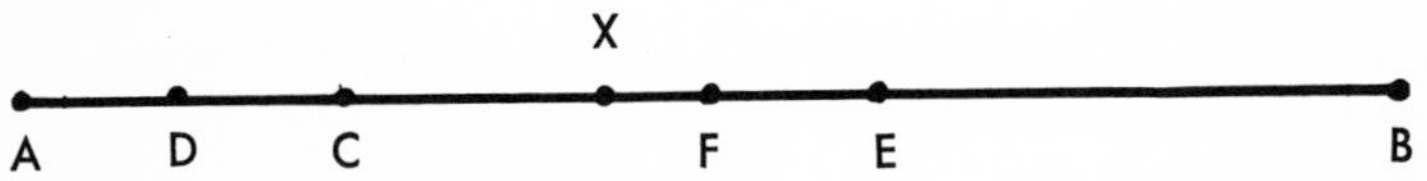

Like other puzzles in this collection, the following depends upon method: it is fairly simple to solve algebraically, but it is required to do it and give proof without construction lines, and by means of geometrical statements only.

On the straight line AB place C anywhere: then place D so that AD = CD; then place E so that CE = BE; and F so that AF = BF; and finally place X so that CX = 2FX.

Prove that BX = 2DX, and AX = 2EX.

Answer on page 110

41

Identifications

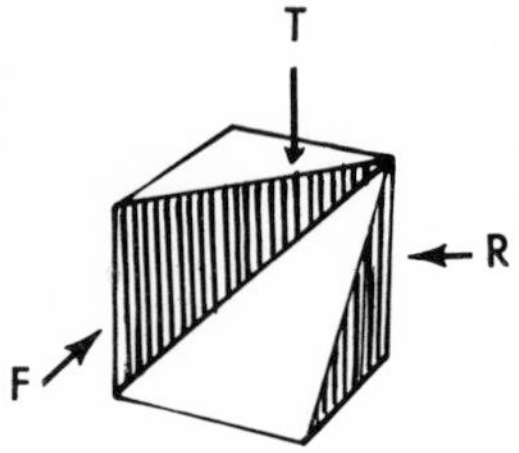

Fig. 1

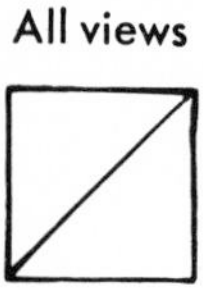

Fig. 2

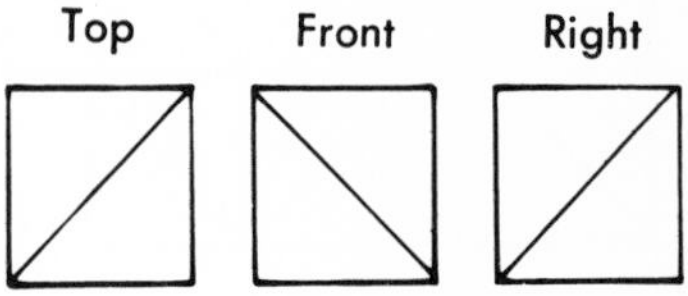

Fig. 3

Architectural plans and projections are examples of orthographic projections—without perspective—from which we can recognize what is represented. But certain arbitrary forms are less easy to identify. Fig. 1 shows in perspective a cube with a triangular wedge cut out of it, and the three orthographic projections from the front, top and right would all be Fig. 2. Had we only seen the latter it might be hard to solve. Fig. 3 shows the three views as labeled, of another form, and the first problem is to identify it. The rules are that a line signifies only a polyhedral edge, like the ones above—never the edge of a plane without thickness, or an isolated geometrical line, like a wire. (Also, if an edge is hidden in any view, it must be shown dotted.) The surfaces may be curved, but in the ones we consider, they are *all flat*.

Answer on page 122

42

The Mayan Pyramids

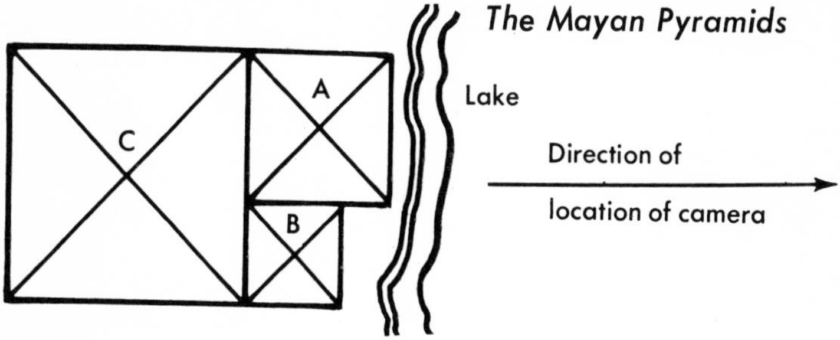

Three Mayan pyramids were recently discovered in Tabasco, and are remarkable for both plan and elevation: they are arranged touching as in the above plan, and are unusually low pitched: the angle formed by their sides is only 30° with the horizontal. After determining this, the discoverer took a photograph of them from across the lake to show their reflection in the still water. He used a telephoto lens and was far enough away so that pyramids A and B were exactly outlined by pyramid C. The camera was at the surface of the water. These circumstances combined to give a practically orthographic projection of pyramids and reflection, without any measurable foreshortening or perspective.

Giving proof, describe the triangle formed by the apexes of the smaller pyramids, A and B, and the reflection of the apex of C, the large one, on the lake in the photograph.

Answer on page 123

43

Speed Test

This is another puzzle with a time limit. Complete this equation:

$$\frac{1234567890}{1234567891^2 - (1234567890 \times 1234567892)} = ?$$

(No computers allowed) Time limit: 4 minutes.

Answer on page 125

44

Two Tombstones

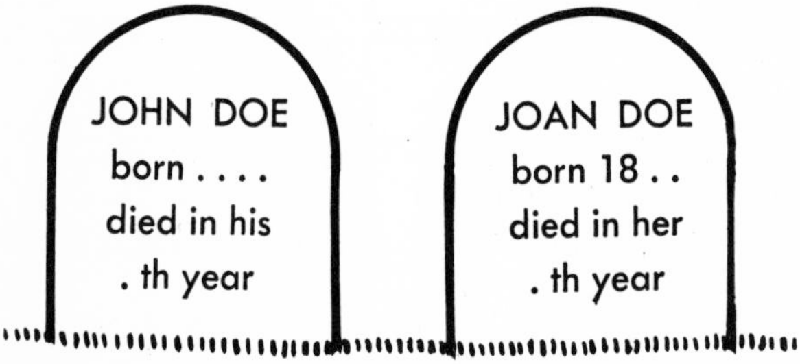
JOHN DOE
born . . . .
died in his
. th year
JOAN DOE
born 18 . .
died in her
. th year

In a churchyard are these two gravestones, parts of which are indecipherable, and indicated here by dots. Family letters show that both Joan and her brother John died in childhood, and that the single missing digit in the bottom line of John's marker was one less than the single digit on Joan's. However, despite this, John lived *longer* than Joan. There are no misstatements in either the inscriptions or family letters. Give the complete *birth year* on one of the stones, within three years.

Answer on page 111

45

The Great Currency Swindle

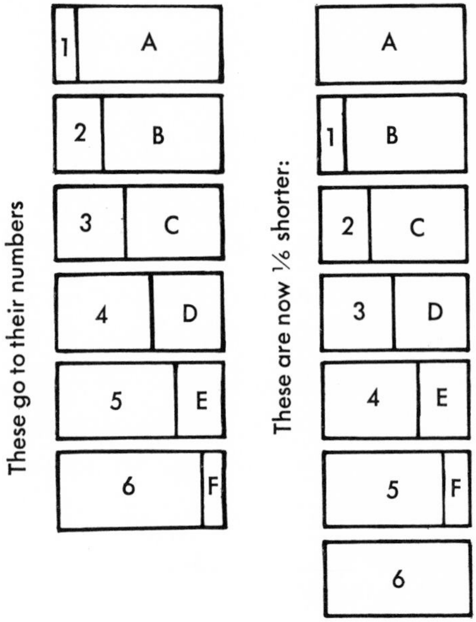

There is a well-known type of trick, or paradox, called a Geometrical Vanish, in which a group of similarly shaped objects—usually made from paper—are cut and manipulated so that one of them seems to disappear. We are here concerned with the reverse: in which an extra object appears out of thin air. The trick has been used by swindlers to make, say, 51 greenbacks out of 50, by cutting and taping them together, as in the figure, which is simplified to 6 bills in this case. (Taping together an "accidentally" cut bill is legal, although banks are suspicious.) The cuts are as shown, each a little further to the right of its predecessor. Then all the left-hand pieces are moved down one and taped to the right-hand parts. The idea is that, if the amount lost in each bill is small enough, it will not be noticed, and an extra one will eventuate. But paper money is numbered, and the serial numbers are all different,* and the miscreant plans to turn them all in at the same time, and the bank would notice any duplications. Also he can only get the bills in a group of successive numbers, and *the number of digits per bill* may vary. The number of bills involved may be increased, so that the cuts will be still closer together. What is his best strategy to make an "extra" bill with an unduplicated number? Will it work? *What will be the number of the new bill?*

Answer on page 115

* For the sake of this puzzle we imagine we are in a country whose bills are numbered once only, not at both ends as U.S. currency is.

46

The Frog and the Angle

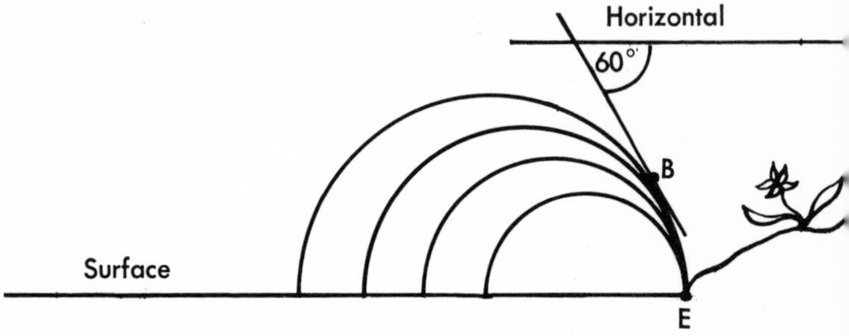

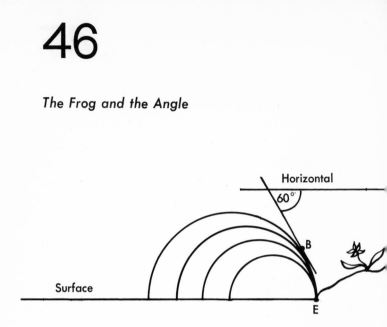

A frog is in a pond, with his eye E at the surface and at the edge of the water. He is blowing a bubble which, as it grows, remains an exact hemisphere (frog-breath contains just enough hydrogen to do it) and, being at the edge of the pond, can only expand to the left, as shown above by the series of semicircles. There is a minute water bug who maintains his position at a point B, where the surface of the bubble is at 60° to the horizontal, and always on a vertical arc through E. The frog is keeping his eye on this maneuver. The question is: Does the angle at which the frog sees the bug increase or decrease as the bubble grows?

The answer can be got without pencil and paper.

Answer on page 126

47

Sliding Triangle

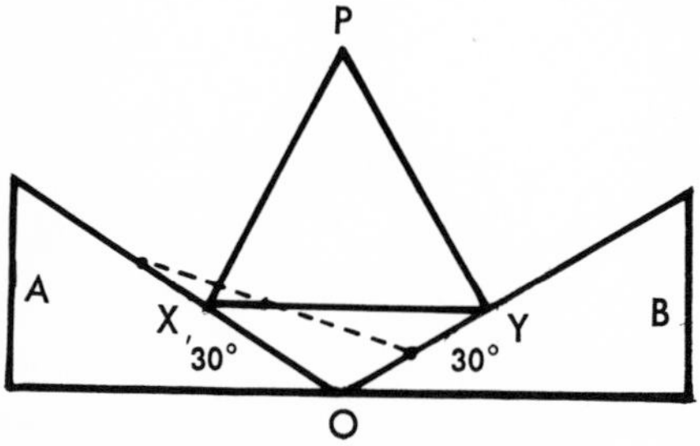

An equilateral triangular block, PXY, sits on the V-shaped arrangement of two blocks A and B. It is free to slide on the inclined planes, which are at 30 degrees to the horizontal, so that its base can tilt either way, e.g., the dotted line. The limits are when X is at O, and when Y is at O.

What path does P describe when the block moves from one extreme to the other? (Give proof.*)

Answer on page 103

* There are various proofs of this solution, one of which we have used earlier.

48

The Short Finger

Comparison of X-ray photographs has shown that the little finger of a man's left hand is very slightly shorter than the one on his right hand, but it is too slight to be detectable by comparing them palm to palm. However, by appropriate comparison of his fingers held tip to tip, he can detect a lesser pressure due to the shortness. Using his hands only, what is the procedure whereby he can ensure the finding of the short finger in the least number of comparisons? What is the minimum number?

Answer on page 130

49

The Fuel Pipe

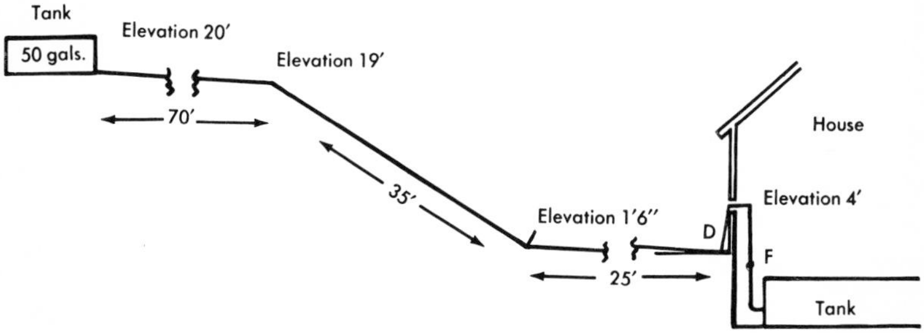

This is a diagrammatic representation of a fuel supply system, with oil tank near the road and lead-in pipe to the house down the hill. It is not drawn to scale, but dimensions and elevations above the level D are correctly given. The upper tank holds 50 gallons, and the pipe holds a gallon per 10 feet. When oil is delivered, the faucet F is closed, so that the upper tank and the pipe are filled. When the lower tank is empty, and the faucet is opened, how much oil gets into the house?

Answer on page 104

50

Paragraph Endings

A manuscript has been typed on narrow pages. There is a certain number of paragraph endings, which will remain unaltered when the text is printed on wider pages, because regardless of width there will always be the same number of paragraphs. But, since the pages are wider, the total number of lines will be reduced, so the ratio of paragraph endings to full lines will be increased.

In some cases in the manuscript, the paragraph endings happen to come at the end of a full line, and the question is: Will the proportion of these occurrences tend to increase, decrease or neither, when the text is printed?

Answer on page 131

51

Terminal Digit Series

Consider the series 1^1, 2^2, 3^3, 4^4 . . . etc. Write down the integers equaling these terms: 1, 4, 27, 256 . . . etc. The terminal digits of these give the series 1, 4, 7, 6 . . .

What is the latter series carried on indefinitely? In other words: What is the series formed by the terminal digits of the integers which equal n^n, when n signifies the integers from 1 taken in order?

Answer on page 134

52

Trapezoid Areas

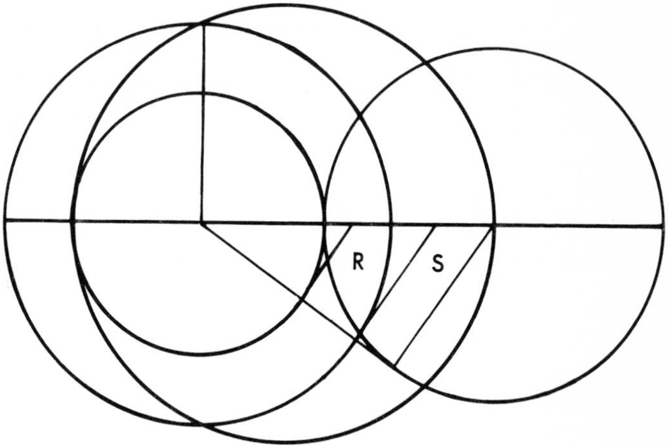

In this figure things are what they seem: The circles have their centers on the long line, and they are where they appear to be; what seem to be right angles are; lines that look like tangents to circles are; where things appear to meet they do. And so forth.

Find the ratio of the areas of the trapezoids, R and S, giving proof. The only theorems necessary are in Euclid.

Answer on page 128

53

Cut Moebius Strips

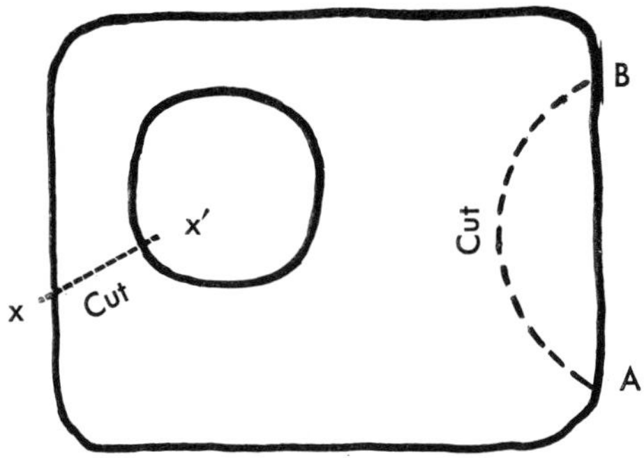

Fig. 1

In topological surfaces a *cross-cut* is defined as one that starts at an edge and finishes at an edge—possibly the same edge—without meeting or crossing itself. In this case an edge is counted as *one* even if it turns a corner: a rectangle of paper has one edge. If there is a hole in the paper it has 2 (disconnected) edges, Fig. 1. It is obvious that if a cross-cut goes from A to B it dissects the paper, but from x to x′ it does not. From this it might seem that the rule is: From edge to same edge dissects; but from one edge to another does not.

(*Continued*)

53 *Continued*

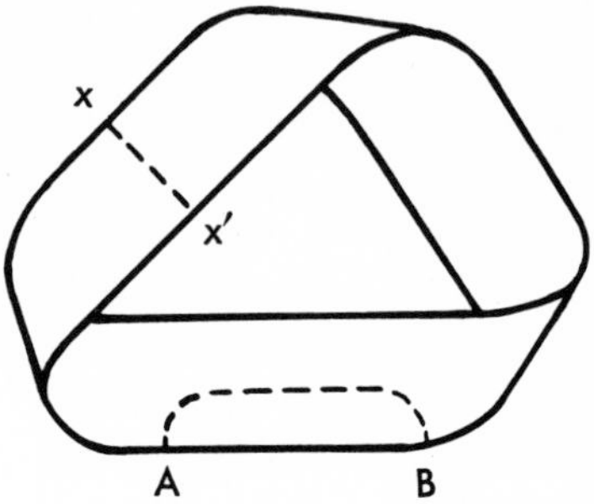

Fig. 2

At first sight the same appears to be true with a Moebius strip, Fig. 2: A to B dissects it; x to x′ does not. But something is odd about it: this surface has *only one edge,* so both cuts shown accord to the first definition: they start at the edge and finish at the same edge.

Imagine that we move B, the finish point of the cross-cut, gradually along the edge. At what place will it allow the cross-cut to end without dissecting the strip? Or, put differently, if we start with the cut x-x′, and gradually move x′, at what point will the cut start dissecting the strip? Keep in mind that the strip has only one side, also.

Answer on page 132

54

The Handicapped Draftsman

A man was about to construct an equilateral triangle, and he had a rectangular drawing board and T-square—enabling him to draw right angles—a compass and a straight-edged strip on which linear distances could be marked off. He had no other instruments. After working for a short time, he used the compass for the first time, and made *one* arc of a circle. Then someone took away the compass. How did he make the triangle?

Answer on page 140

55

Dividing the Moebius Strip

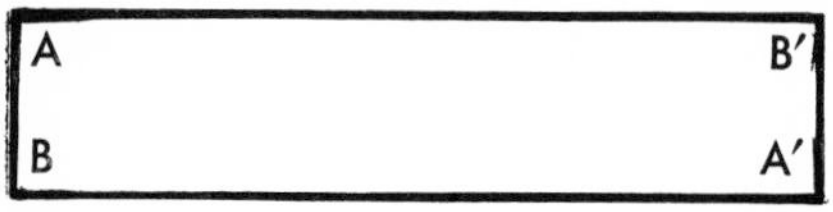

Fig. 1

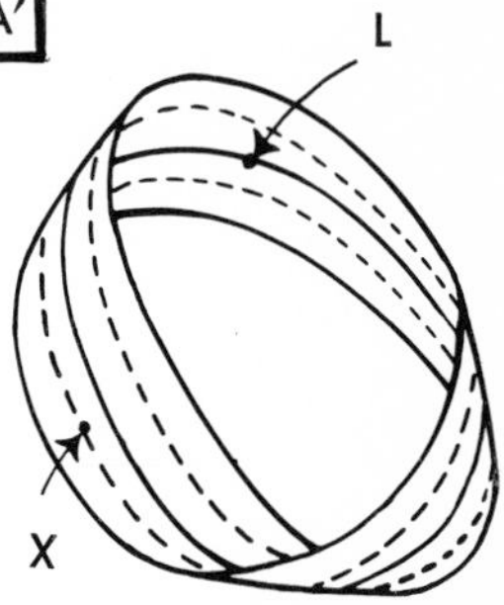

Fig. 2

Make a Moebius strip from a piece of paper (Fig. 1), which is given a half-twist and then joined end to end, so that A is joined to A′ and B to B′, as in Fig. 2. It has only one edge, as can be seen by following it with the eye, and only one side, as can be proved by drawing a line L along the center; L will be on both "sides." If the strip is cut along this line L it remains in one piece, not surprisingly since the top half, A-B′, has been joined to the bottom half, B-A′. If it is cut along the dotted line, X, it comes apart in two unequal loops.

The problem is to draw one straight line on the strip which starts *at the edge,* so that when the strip is cut along the line it will be divided into two pieces of *equal area.* Prove it.

Answer on page 141

56

Hokusai's Garden

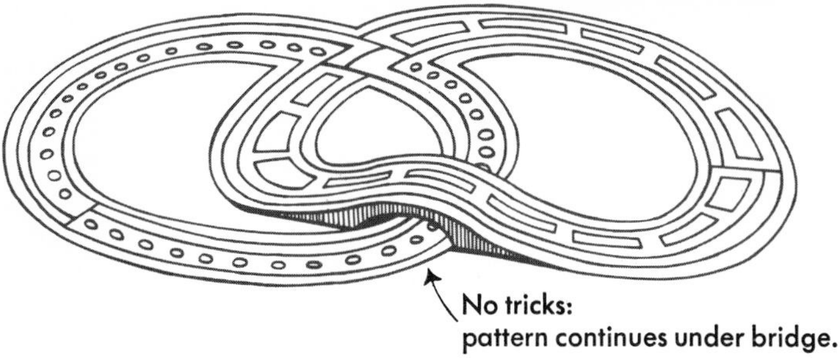
No tricks:
pattern continues under bridge.

Hokusai had a garden. "Japanese garden," he said, "should have little stone bridge." Being a famous artist, he designed it so that the bridge went over a path instead of a stream, as shown here. The two looped paths were to be laid out in strips of unglazed tile. Now, as everybody knows—although it hasn't been proved—a map of the world or any imaginary country can be colored with four colors so that no two regions having a common boundary will have the same color. Hokusai's young friend, Hiroshige, suggested that the tiles would look nice if they were colored like a map: no two of the same color touching. It can readily be seen that the outside and inside strips of both loops together form one continuous area, and one color will do for that. The problem is to color the drawing—or number the areas—using the fewest possible number of colors, and give a thoroughgoing technical explanation for the number needed.

Answer on page 143

57

The Square Pizza

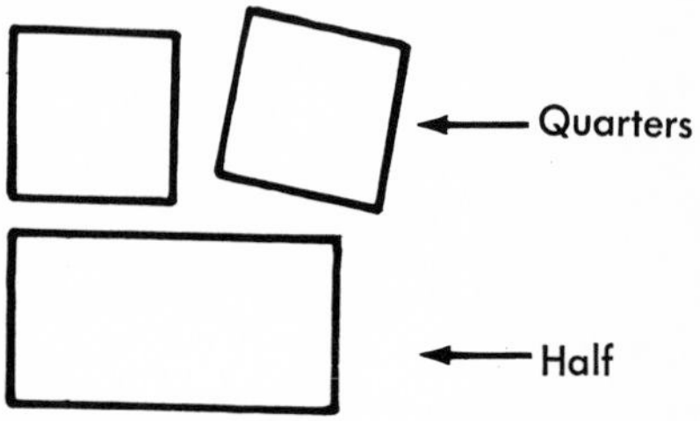

A civic-minded girl has a large square pizza (from a Chinese pizzeria) which she plans to share with three friends, so she has cut it in half, and then cut one of the halves in half, with the intention of then cutting the as-yet-uncut half in two. The figure shows what she has done, when one of her three friends says that she doesn't like pizza. This changes things. Question (to be answered in the head): She now wants the pizza to be in three equal shares, so in how few (straight) cuts can she attain this, and where do the cuts go?

Answer on page 131

58

Two Mirrors

A man is sitting in a large office looking at a wall mirror, A, which is in front of him. *Behind* him is a stenographer who is reflected in first another mirror, B, parallel to A, and that reflection is seen (by the man) reflected in A. This secondary reflection does not, of course, reverse the stenographer from left to right, as the primary reflection in B does. She is at that moment in actuality moving away from the man, he observes the odd fact that the secondary reflection of her in A is *also* moving away from him. How are the mirrors arranged? If necessary, give a diagram. ("Parallel" means within 5°.)

Answer on page 102

59

Section of Cube

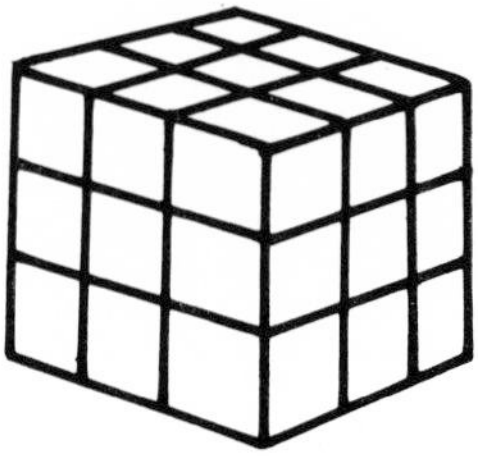

A carpenter, working with a band saw, wants to cut a 3-inch wooden cube into 27 1-inch cubes; as seen in the figure, it can be done with six cuts. Question: Can he reduce the number of necessary cuts by rearranging the pieces after each cut? How?

This puzzle was stated in substantially the above terms in Martin Gardner's Mathematical Games department in *Scientific American*, and the answer given was that it is impossible to do it in less than six cuts, since the center 1-inch cube will have six faces newly cut, and the saw must make "six passes." Proofs of this, and more general versions, were mentioned as having been worked out by various distinguished mathematicians. Nevertheless we rather presumptuously pose the problem again.

Answer on page 146

60

Box and Curve

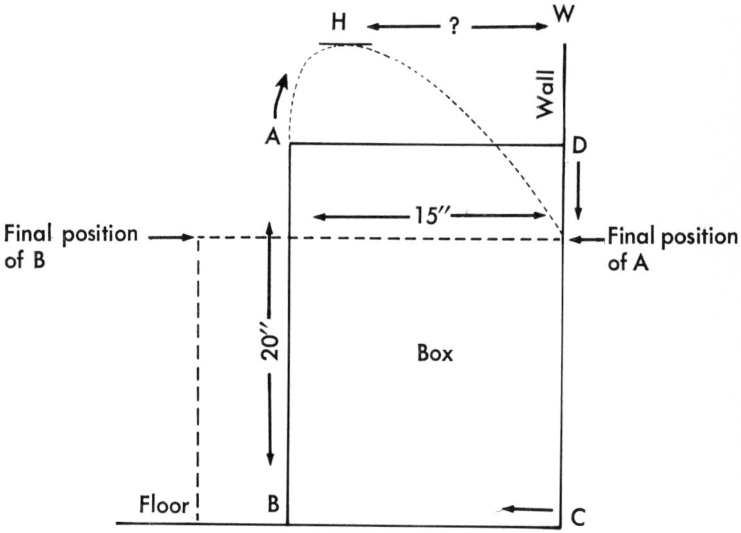

A rectangular box, 20 inches high and 15 inches from front to back, sits on the floor against a wall, W. A man pulls out the bottom of the box but holds the top against the wall, so that the edge C slides forward along the floor, and D slides down against the wall, as shown by the arrows. The top front edge, A, describes an upward, inward and then downward curve as shown, stopping when the box is flat on the floor. How far is H, the high point of the curve, from the wall? (Time limit, 3 minutes.)

Answer on page 139

61

The Torquous

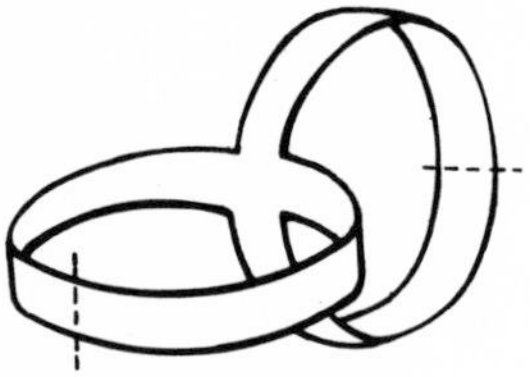

Fig. 1

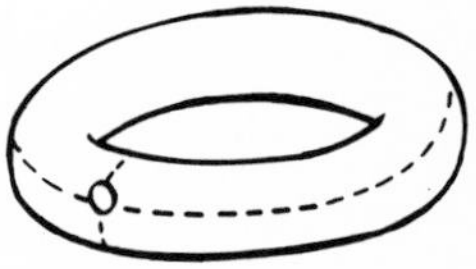

Fig. 2

In Puzzle 56, Hokusai's garden was seen to be the equivalent of a torus with a single puncture, which gave it one edge—an unpunctured torus has no edge, like an inner tube without the air hole. Fig. 1 shows one of the stages in enlarging the puncture; the surface still retains these characteristics of a punctured torus: (1) two sides; (2) one edge; (3) the possibility of a map needing seven colors; and (4) a *Betti number of 2*. For our purposes, the latter can be defined as the number

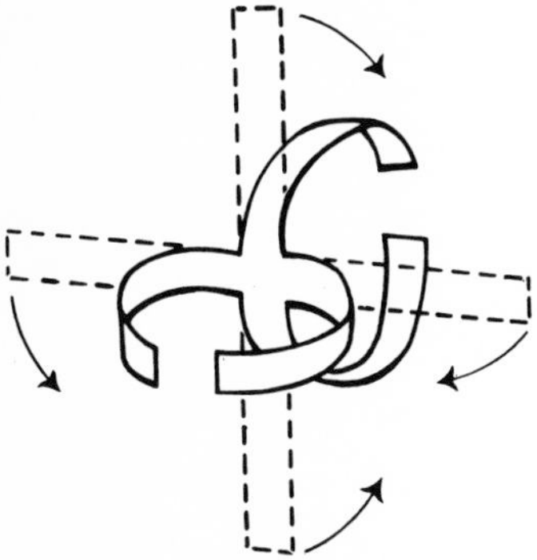

Fig. 3

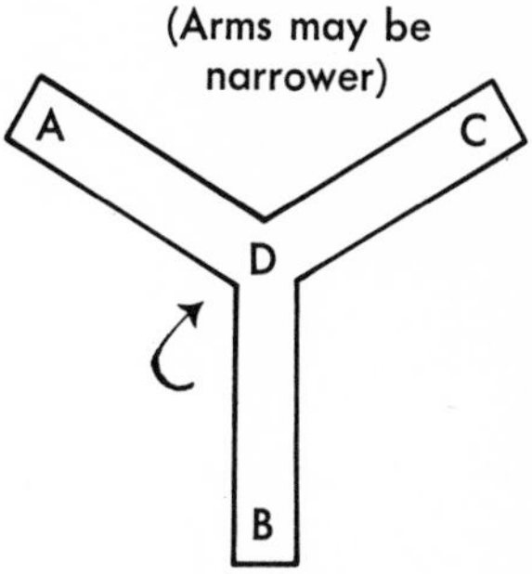

Fig. 4

of cross-cuts (see Puzzle 53) that can be made without cutting the torus apart. Fig. 2 shows an undistorted punctured torus, and the dotted lines are two cross-cuts we can make without dissecting it, and the dotted lines in Fig. 1 are their equivalent. The latter can be made from a paper cross, Fig. 3, and the first part of this puzzle is to make from the three-armed piece in Fig. 4 a form that will have the same four characteristics listed above, and be *symmetrical about an axis:* e.g., it would not do just to join A to B, and C over and around to D, as it would give an asymmetric version of Fig. 1.

Answer on page 144

62

Bughouse Binary

At one time people used a double negative for emphasis, but when the Revival of Learning took hold, a more mathematical meaning was assigned to it, and, the way things stand now, Two Negatives Equal a Positive. One might think that therefore two positives equal a negative, but perhaps owing to the fact that Samuel Johnson was given to extreme positiveness, such is not the case: they, also, equal a positive. On the other hand, a combination of positive and negative gives a negative, regardless of their order: "My answer *is* No!" and "My answer is *not* Yes!" Both mean *No.*

Mathematical logic seems to have taken these rules to heart: $-1 \times -1 = +1$; $+1 \times +1 = +1$; $+1 \times -1$

Continued 62

$= -1$ and $-1 \times +1 = -1$. These relationships can be thought of in a slightly different way if we call the elements Agree and Disagree; we can represent them by 1 = agreement and 0 = disagreement, and the rules will stay the same: 0,0 = 1; 1,1 = 1; 1,0 = 0 and 0,1 = 0. Let us start a row of these symbols—quite arbitrarily—and put down a 1, and under it to the left another 1: $\begin{matrix} & 1 \\ 1 & \end{matrix}$. In the space to the right of the lower 1 we then put another 1, indicating that the 1's agree: $\begin{matrix} & 1 \\ 1 & 1 \end{matrix}$ and if we had a continuing row of 1's along the top, and kept filling in the lower row according to the rule, we would have this: $\begin{matrix} \;1111111\ldots \\ 11111111\ldots \end{matrix}$ Very dull. But if we started instead with 0's on the top, we'd get: $\begin{matrix} \;00000000\ldots \\ 010101010\ldots \end{matrix}$ since the *first* 1, which indicates the agreement of the first two 0's, *disagrees* with the next 0 above, and calls for a 0, which in turn *agrees* with the next 0 above, and so on, alternating *ad infinitum.*

Question 1. If we keep adding new rows below the rows we already have, like this third:

$$\begin{matrix} \;00000\ldots \\ 010101\ldots \\ 001100\ldots \end{matrix}$$

(always starting with a 0), how far must we carry on to get a repeating pattern *all over*—like wallpaper?

Answer on page 152

Answers

2

Answer

BD = the horizontal length of the lower front.

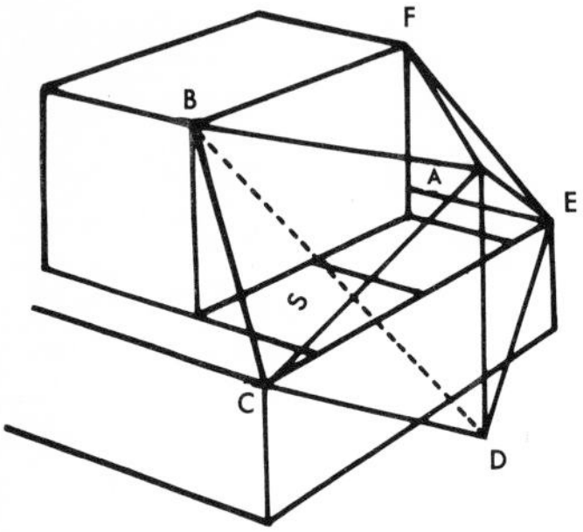

Fig. 1

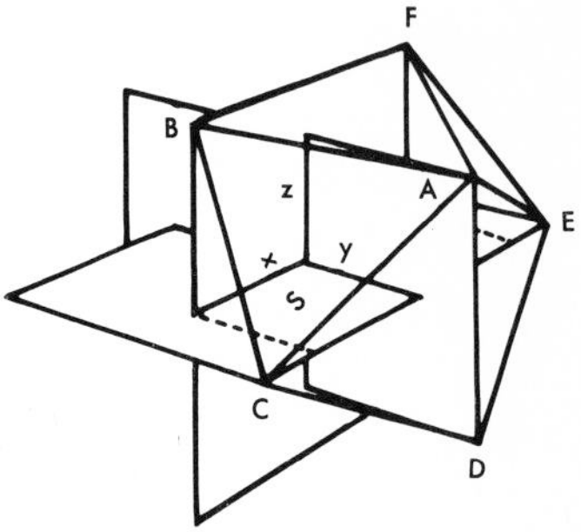

Fig. 2

The key is symmetry, and the proportions of the roof garden. By the symmetry of flagpole and facade, triangles ABC, ACD, ADE, AEF, and AFB are equal and equilateral, Fig. 1, but this alone does not prove they form a regular pentagonal pyramid; even with AD vertical, the dihedral angles are variable. But the roof garden measures 1 x 2: we imagine a center line through it in line with the pole. The nearer half is a square, S, and the point C being in a line with the front edge of it uniquely determines the pyramid to be regular. Thus BD = CE. Here is the reason:

Continued 2

Fig. 2 shows the three equal rectangles whose corners coincide with the 12 vertices of a regular icosahedron. They intersect one another at right angles symmetrically at x, y and z. We know that x and y are sides of a square; $x = \frac{1}{2}$ BF $= \frac{1}{2}$ AD, so $x = y = z$ (since $z = \frac{1}{2}$ AD). The fact that these rectangles are in the "extreme and mean" proportion, expressed by the symbol phi, ϕ, is not needed here: only that the pyramid ABCDEF is regular. With the above given, it is.

9

Answer

The wolf should go in, kill a sheep and tear it into pieces—as he normally would to eat it. Then he should poke the pieces through the bars and go out and eat them.

3

Answer

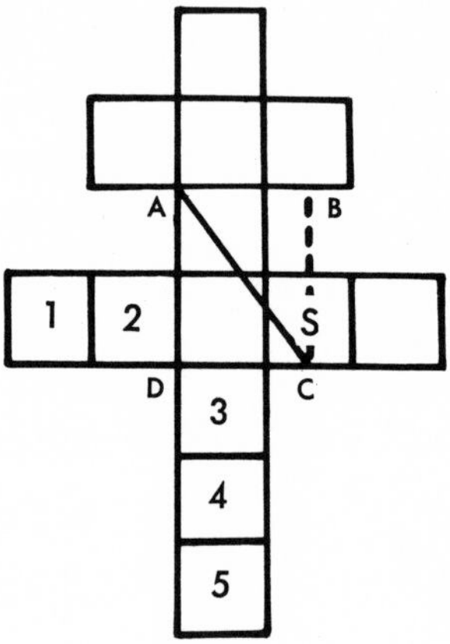

The cut is AC, where C is the center point of the bottom of square S.

Proof: Draw BC parallel to AD. Triangle ADC is ½ the area of rectangle ABCD and, since AB = 1½ and AD = 2, the area of ABCD = 3. Thus the area of triangle ADC = 1½. This, added to the numbered squares, is 6½, which is half the total area, 13.

15

Answer

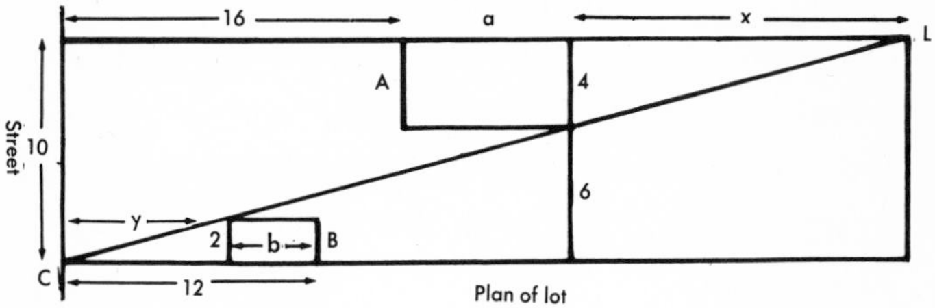

Plan of lot

The lot is 40 yards deep. “Just get a glimpse” means that Pete sees the lamp, L, from the corner C. If a and b were less, it would be more than a glimpse; if greater, L could not be seen at all. Substitute the known dimensions in the plan above.

By similar triangles, $\frac{12 - b}{2} = \frac{16 + a}{6}$

Therefore, multiplying by 2, $12 - b = \frac{16 + a}{3}$

Or, $36 - 3b = 16 + a$

Since the sheds are similar, and 4 is twice 2, $a = 2b$

Substituting, $36 - 3b = 16 + 2b$

Thus $b = 4; a = 8$

By similar triangles, $x = 2y$

And, since $y = 12 - b = 8$, $x = 16$

Therefore the length of the lot is $16 + a + x = 40.$

4

Answer

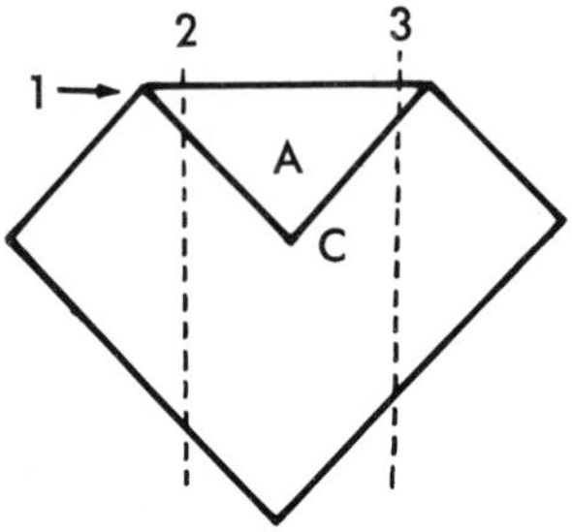

Fig. 1

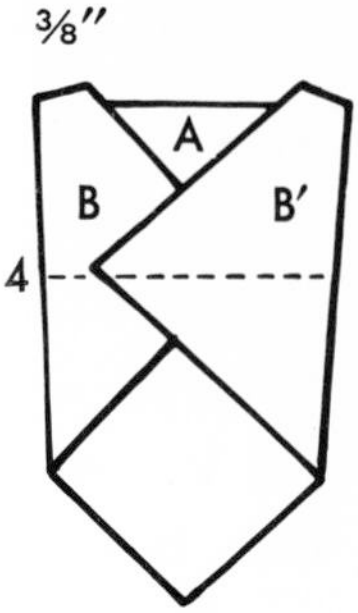

Fig. 2

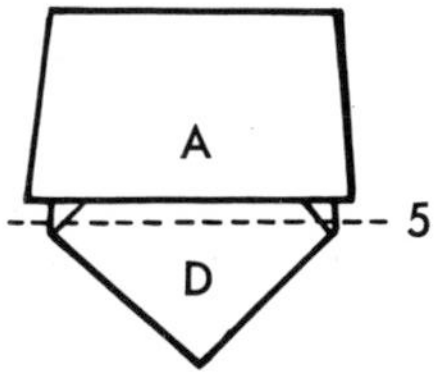

Fig. 3

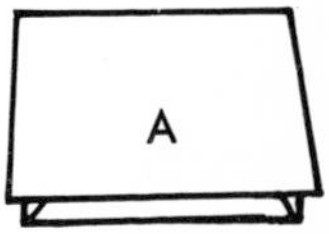

Fig. 4

Five folds.

First fold top A to center point C. Then the sides B and B′ are folded in on the dotted lines 2 and 3 in Fig. 1. These are ⅜ inch from the ends of the first fold, but tilted together at the bottom—about ⅛ inch closer, giving Fig. 2. Then fold the top down on horizontal fold 4 which runs through C, getting Fig. 3. Then fold the bottom triangle D up on line 5, which is ⅛ inch below A. Make a crease and open the triangle out again. Then tuck D *into* A, so that it is under the main part of A but over the folded-in sides B and B′.

10

Answer

Animal A could be a lion, who can do 100 yards at about 45 mph, in a series of bounds. Then he slows down to a mere 20 mph, and then less. Animal B could be a wolf, who cannot do more than 25 or 30 mph, but can keep it up for hours. The lion can catch him at once; he can catch the lion eventually. (Or a *man* and a *horse*.)

6

Answer

Zero. The rope breaks the moment he lets go of the loop and the spike holds it, because when this happens the stress is doubled—and, as we said, the rope was at 90% of its breaking point.

5

Answer

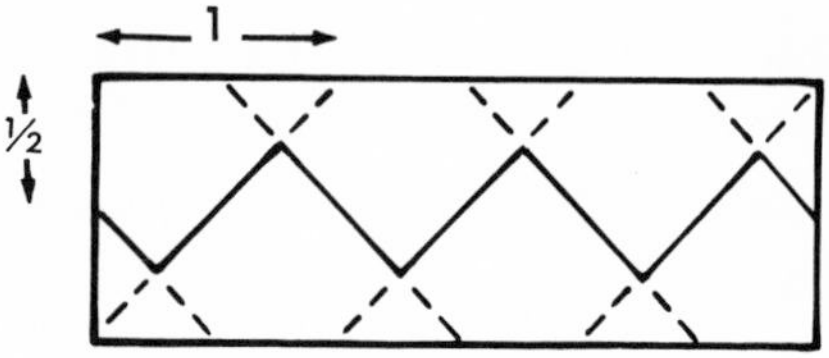

Solid lines = cuts

Fig. 1

All angles at 45°

Dotted lines = folds

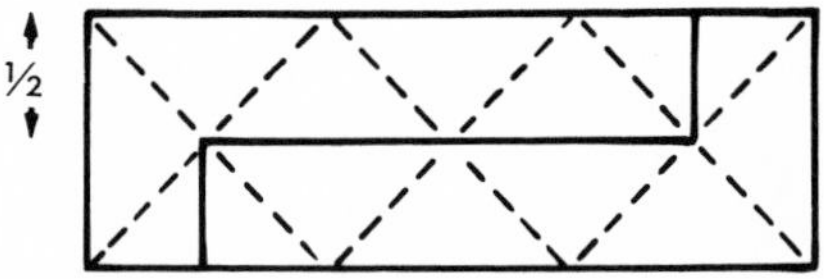

Fig. 2

These are the two basic answers—the second and more elegant being discovered by Alison Ames, of Woodstock, New York. An infinite series of variations of these—forming two families—was discovered by C. L. Baker of Bethesda, Maryland, and published in *Recreational Mathematics Magazine*, June 1962. To form the latter solutions we distort the cutting lines (but not the folds) in a kind of mirrored pattern—too complicated to go into here.

16

Answer

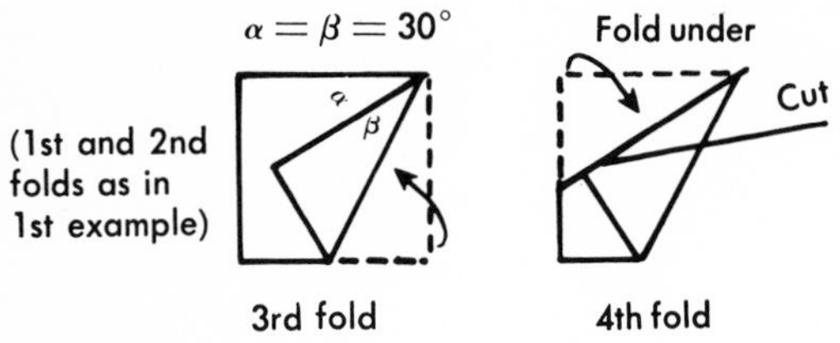

Fig. 1

Fig. 2

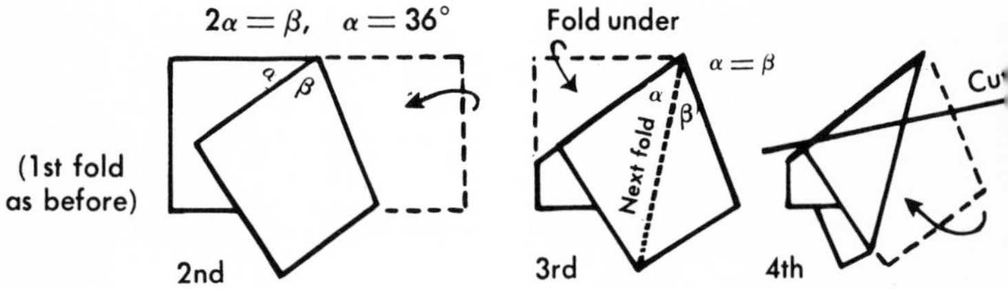

Fig. 3

Problem A: The easier one is six-pointed, with the folds shown in Fig. 1; the resulting star in Fig. 2.

The five-pointed star is more complicated—folds in Fig. 3; resulting star in Fig. 4. (*Continued*)

16 *Continued*

Problem B: Make the first *two* folds of Fig. 7 in the questions. Cut at right angles to the center part of the first-made fold (angle α in Fig. 5). This gives an equilateral triangle (Fig. 6). Since its angles are acute, it is a star by the given definition.

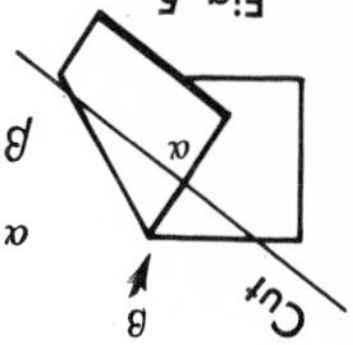

$\alpha = 90°$

$\beta = 60°$

Fig. 5

Fig. 4

Fig. 6

13

Answer

The square gives 3 and the triangle gives 4 turns.

18

Answer

100 feet, because flags 1 and 3 are opposite. Call the distances (as shown in the sketch) A, B, and C:

1. A is to B as B is to A + B, or

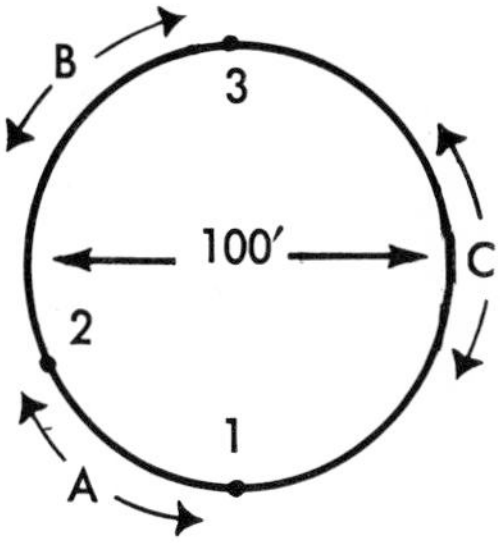

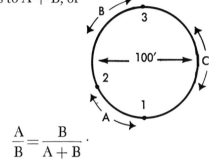

$$\frac{A}{B} = \frac{B}{A+B}.$$

This ratio is the Golden Section, or *Divina Proportione,* symbolized by phi (ϕ), and since the same ratio pertains to B and C, A is to B as B is to C. Therefore:

2. $$\frac{A}{B} = \frac{B}{C}.$$

Therefore: $$\frac{B}{A+B} = \frac{B}{C},$$

or $$A + B = C.$$

The mathematical friend didn't even have to work out the above; he made use of the fact that in any series of values with the ratio of ϕ between adjacent terms, any term is the sum of the previous two, in this case $C = A + B$. ($\phi = 1.61803398\ldots$ etc.)

14

Answer

A gives 3, B gives 2. Spills 1 and 4 are got by rolling the strip away from us. For example:

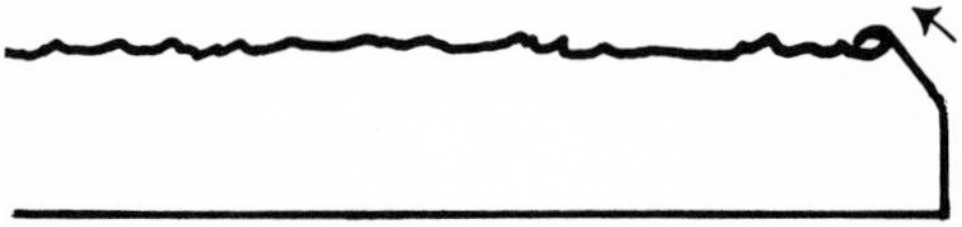

(Gives 1)

19

Answer

1. *Caveat emptor* (Latin, like "pro tem").
2. *Ctenoid* (means comb-edged; it is in most desk dictionaries).
3. *Counterclockwise* (an example of nonwisdom).

27

Answer

From 1 pound to infinity. It is 1 pound, *not* 2, because when the length approaches infinity the second weight converges to zero. When the hidden rod's length is zero the weight must be infinite to balance the 1 foot-pound force on the left.

24

Answer

```
    99
    99
   ----
   891
  891
  -----
  9801
   199
 ------
 10000
```

The clue is that there are five digits in the total. Any other digits than 9's in the first two lines and following the "1" given in the question, would give us only four digits in the total.

17

Answer

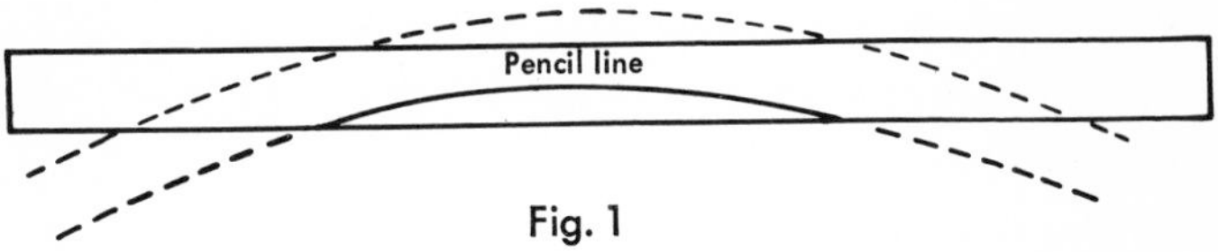

Fig. 1

Fig. 2

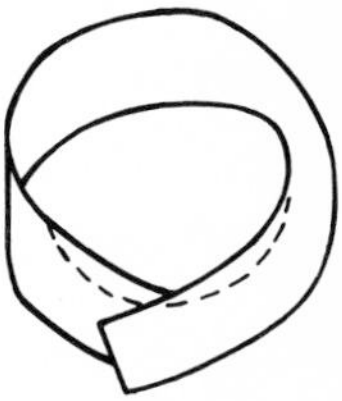

Problem 1: The part of the strip least amenable to being rounded is the twist, so draw a line on it where the circle should come, and open it out, Fig. 1. We cut a new, curved strip (dotted lines), but things are not much improved. If we join the ends *at an angle*, Fig. 2, the hole is rounder. A line drawn to smooth out the angle (dotted line in Fig. 2) suggests an S-curve, and Fig. 3 is the best form. Join by bringing AB over and face-to-face with A′B′. (Draw line L.)

Problem 2: Fig. 5 shows how a loose, unjoined paper cylinder can be put in the hole and allowed to expand. Then the line of contact can be marked and cut, and the upper half joined to the strip. All we need now is a disk for the top. The resultant hat is all right for a doll, but if we have a full-sized doll in mind we want something with more style.

The next problem is to make a hat with the crown and brim in one continuous piece, but approximately parallel like a road: one curved strip. Then, by departing from the rule of parallelism, improve on its looks.

Answers on pages 88–91

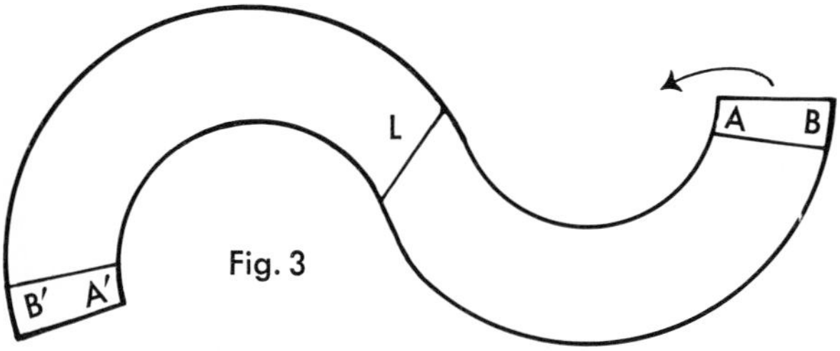

Fig. 3

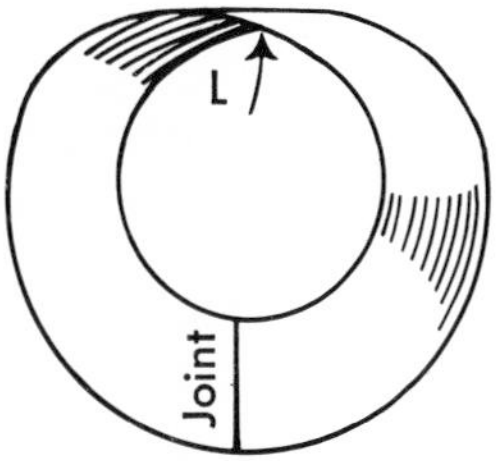

Fig. 4 Top view

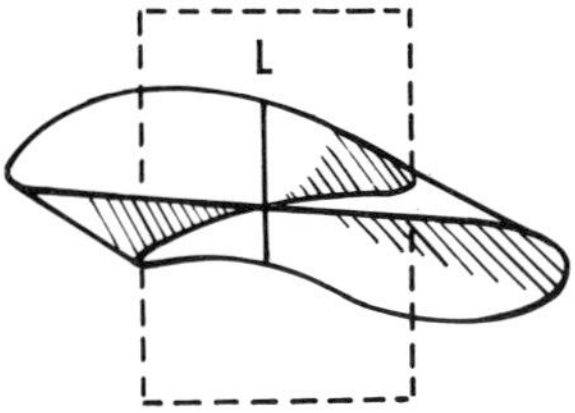

Fig. 5 Front

17a

Answer

Pattern 1: Parallel curved strip: Hold the strip (Fig. 1) with C′J′ facing you. The left-hand part with CJ is turned under and to the right; the right-hand part with AB is turned under and to the left, as shown. Put CJ facing *up* on C′J′, and join. We now have the crown (without its top). Now turn it around to the left so that A′B′ faces you (Fig. 2). Start joining the inner edge of the brim, point A′, to the crown at A″, and continue joining with very small tags of tape (⅛ inch wide, ¼ inch between), until AB lies face-to-face on A′B′. Join them. Trace the outline of the top of the crown onto a (curved) piece of paper; cut and insert.

(*Continued*)

Continued 17a

Fig. 1

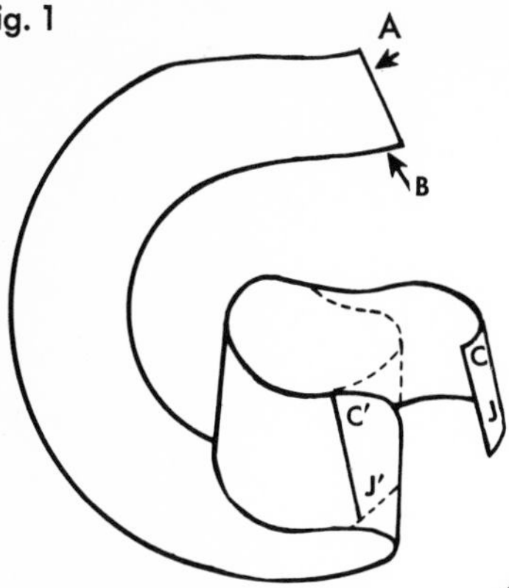

Pattern 1

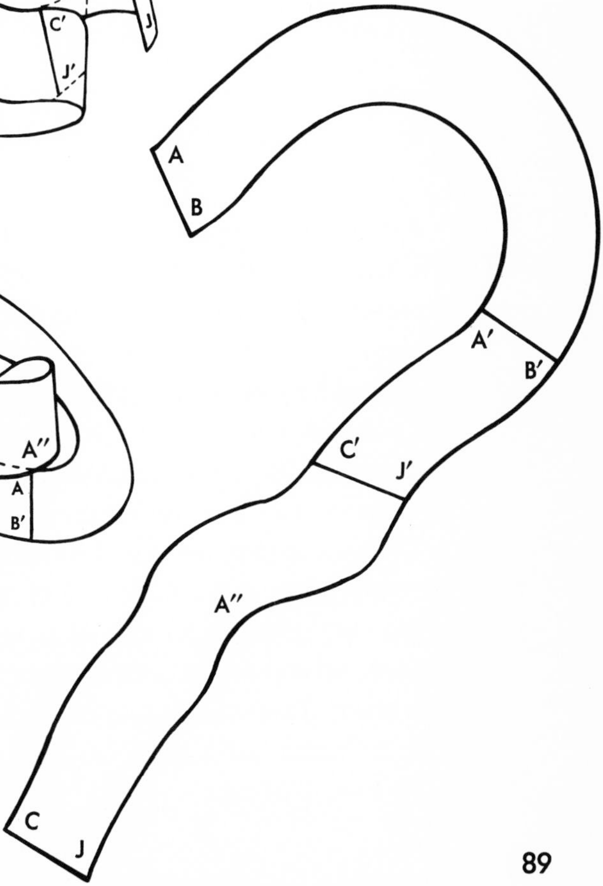

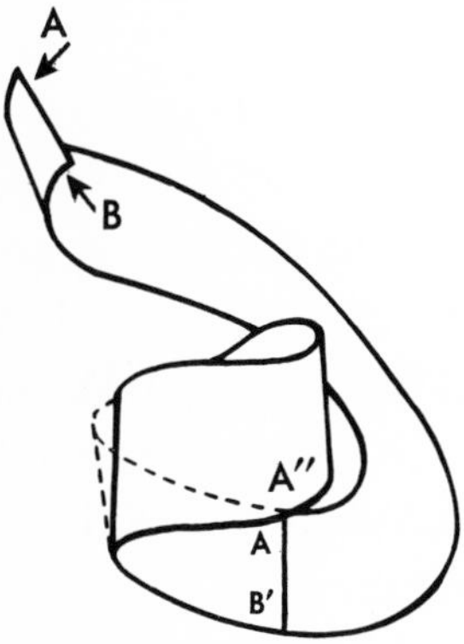

Fig. 2

17a *Continued*

Pattern 2: Variation: Face C′J′ toward you (Fig. 3). The left-hand part is turned under and to the right, and CJ is put face up on C′J′ and joined. Continue as with Pattern 1, joining the inner edge of the brim from A′ to the right, to lower edge of the crown at J. When AB lies face-to-face on A′B′, join. Make and insert the top. If so desired, the upper contour of the crown can be given more of a curve, like Pattern 1.

To make a full-sized hat, take either pattern to a photostat place and ask for a blow-up. Tell them to make the distance X — X whatever head size is wanted: mark it on the pattern: 21¼ inches, or whatever it is. Ask for a *matte* print, take it to your milliner with the above instructions. It can be made from felt, or buckram, covered.

Continued 17a

Pattern 2

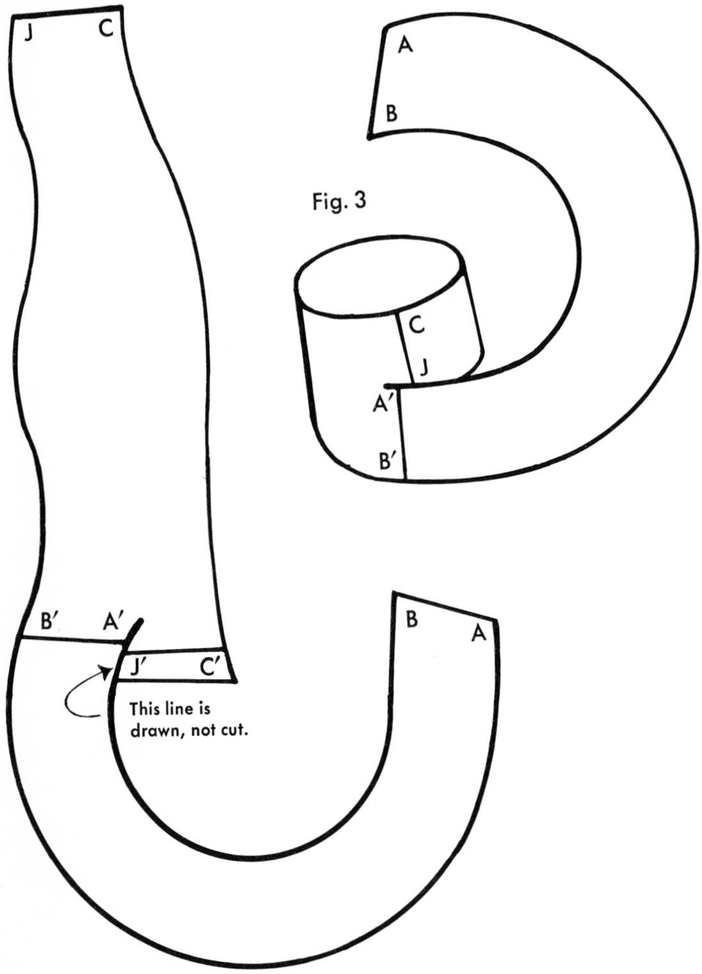

Fig. 3

X —— Make this . . . . . . inches —— X

22

Answer

Such irregularity of growth is inexplicable unless he assumes that there are *two* lashes growing at almost the same place, but with different periodicity. He charts the intervals:

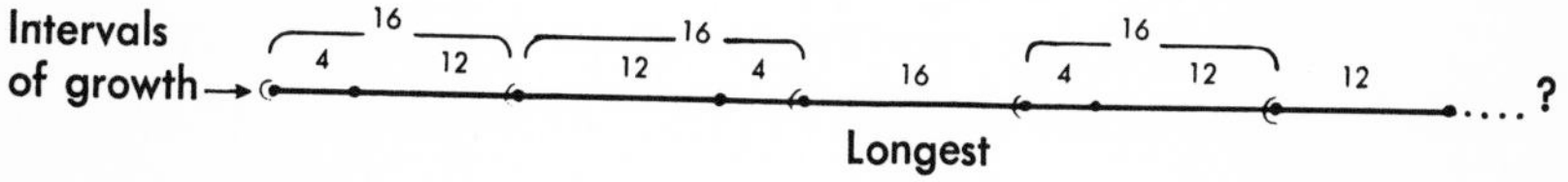

The longest interval, 16 days, must represent an uninterrupted example of a *short* interval—otherwise it would be interrupted by a shorter one. He counts backward and forward from it. Sure enough, there are dates at intervals of 16 days (top line), so he circles them, and sees that the remaining ones are at 24-day intervals. Thus one lash grows every 16 days; the other every 24 days. Extending his chart forwards, he finds the next lash will be one of the short-period ones: 4 days hence.

21

Answer

The figure shows one of the two known ways. The mere placing of a rubber band to conform to the figure is a tricky problem, which we leave to the reader. A hint: Don't bother about the twists while making the arrangement. Once the band is in position it is easy to get rid of them by rolling.

26

Answer

Alphabetical order is abandoned completely. The best arrangement is synthetic; from simple to complex, and making use of two dimensions, which a single list does not do.

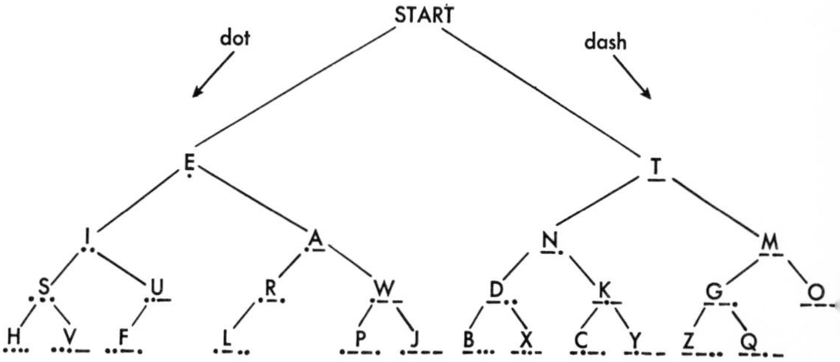

In receiving with this chart, move *down* for each sound; to the *left* for a dot, to the *right* for a dash. Example: down Right, down Left, down Right, reaches K, – · – At a pause—indicating the end of that particular symbol—move instantly back to the starting point, taking note of the last letter stopped at. It is important to get the person who is sending the signals to go slow enough so that *no mistakes are made;* otherwise the receiver will be practicing errors.

Continued 26

With this chart, the more frequently used letters are passed through on the way to the less so, and more complex ones. In this way one unconsciously practices letters like e, t, a, i, o, n and the rest. In following the chart we can use a pointer or just our eyes. Eventually the chart becomes unnecessary. Some people might prefer to make a large copy of it.

--. --- --- -..   .... ..- -. - .. -. --.

28

Answer

A cube. The stellated tetrahedron we began with had 12 faces, but when α becomes 180°, the faces line up in pairs, becoming one face per pair, giving a total of six. Since each of these is composed of two triangles joined, they have four sides each. By definition the tetrahedron was regular and this form is *symmetrical*, so what we now have has six equal four-sided faces which meet at *equal angles*, and all the edges are equal. The only polyhedron that can be so described is a cube. (See figure on page 32.)

32

Answer

From what we know of snow and trees;
It was a light, uneven breeze.

A dead calm would have left things as they were, and not being surrounded by other evergreens, the hemlock must have had its wide lower branches covered by the snow, also. If there had been a strong wind the snow would have been knocked off the top, even more than from the lower parts. With sticky snow and a light gust, things are reversed: the series of gusts dislodge a little (mostly from the top), but these lumps of snow, not being carried away, fall on lower branches, which makes them drop still more, and this falls on still lower ones. Thus a sort of downward-expanding, chain reaction is set up, until practically all the snow is gone from the lowest part. A warm sun might do the same, but the sky was dark. The phenomenon is common, but rarely remarked.

30

Answer

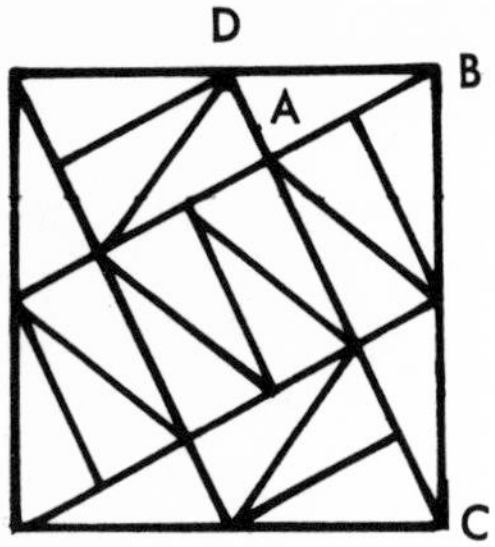

Fig. 1

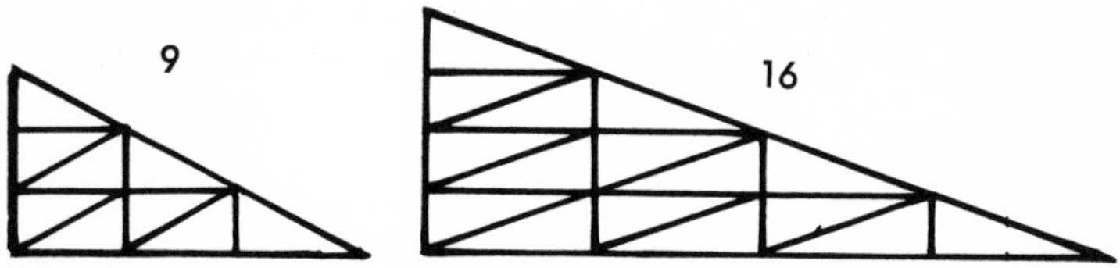

Fig. 2

As in Fig. 1 (with 15 cuts). If we then subdivide every small triangle in the way ABC is cut, we get 80 pieces. Since the process is limitless we can go on to infinity. This gives a series: $4^n \cdot (20)$, where n is the number of times we subdivide the small triangles. We cannot subdivide them into five, as is BCD, because if we did it to ADB, two of the cuts would be parallel to the side BC. However, the triangles can be cut into more pieces: Fig. 2 shows 9 and 16, and this leads to a more general series for the total numbers of pieces; $(x^2)^n \cdot (20)$, where x is any integer. (*Continued*)

30 *Continued*

Fig. 3

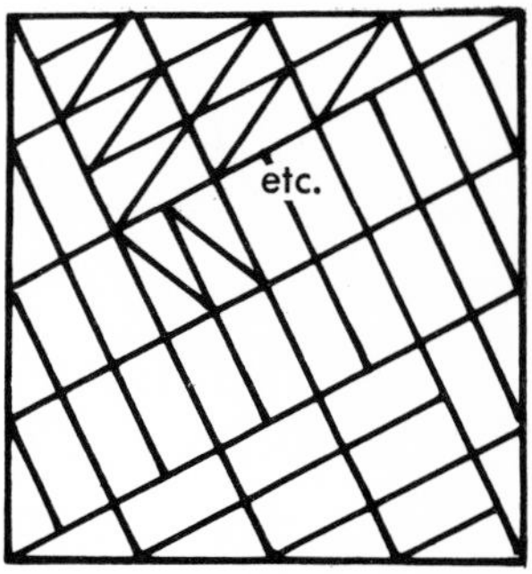

Fig. 4

The whole square can be divided in a different way, too. In Fig. 3 the sides are divided into three, leading to a total of 60 pieces, and thus to a different series. Also, Fig. 1 can be increased as in Fig. 4 by dividing the sides into 4, giving 80 pieces. All the above methods give totals that are multiples of 20.

Second Puzzle: Cut the square so as to get a total that is *not* a multiple of 20.

Answer on page 102

33

Answer

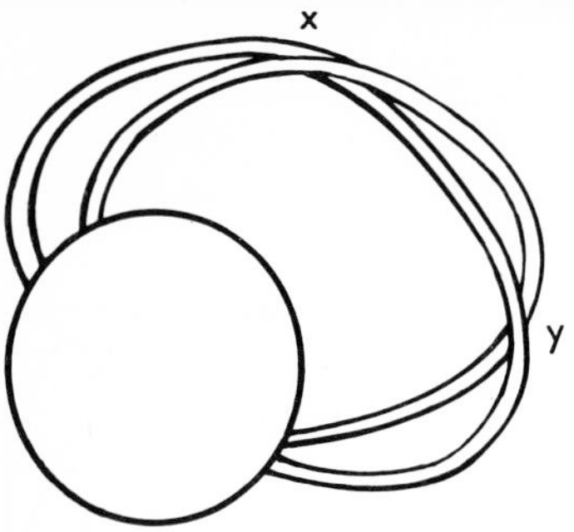

Fig. 1

Fig. 1 shows that there is a crossing of the cord with itself in the same sense as the twists at x and y. It is because a simple, or "overhand," knot in an endless loop is always in the form of a trefoil:

(Remember, Mr. A saw no knot.)

The second question: A *square, or reef, knot.* If the form shown in the question Fig. 2 is made with cord, tightened and pulled into the forms shown here, Fig. 3, the result is clear, but without using cord it is very hard to recognize. Now try making a granny knot the same way.

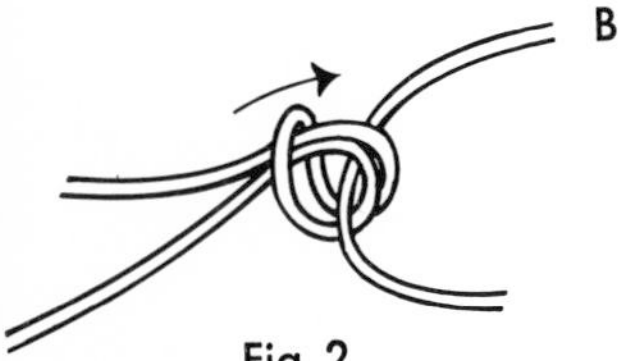

Fig. 2

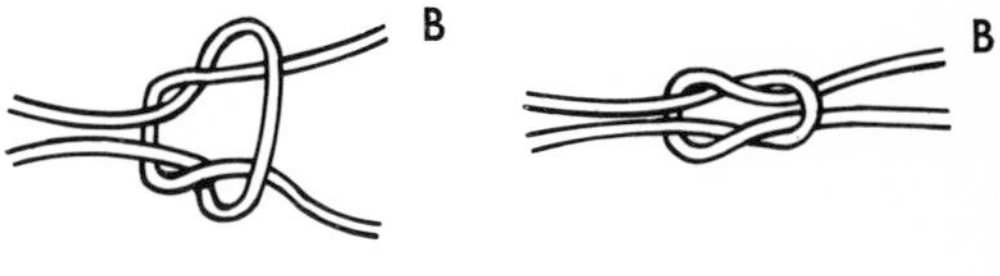

Fig. 3

12

Answer

Unlike a domestic cat a lion has round pupils:

$\therefore$ X = cat or kitten.

Hyenas are of the suborder *Aeluroidea,* which includes the felines (not *Arctoidea,* which includes the dogs), so:

$\therefore$ Y = lion, cat, or kitten.

Since X has never touched Y (mother and child *have* touched),

Y must equal lion.

This can be solved *without* knowing the above, because if you write all the possible combinations of pupil ratio and suborders (four combinations only), the other three give equivocal answers, and it was said that the answer must be unique.

The three other possibilities are shown in the following:

1. Based on the wrong assumption that the lion has a slit-shaped pupil, but with the hyena correctly related.

Lion has slit-shaped pupil,

$\therefore$ X = Great Dane, poodle or puppy.

Hyenas are related to cats,

$\therefore$ Y = lion, cat or kitten.

X has never touched Y,

$\therefore$ Y = lion, cat or kitten.

(Not unique.)

2. Based on the wrong assumption that hyenas are related to dogs, but with the lion's pupil correct.

Lion has round pupils,

$\therefore$ X = cat or kitten.

Hyenas are related to dogs,

$\therefore$ Y = Great Dane, poodle or puppy.

X has never touched Y,

$\therefore$ Y = Great Dane, poodle or puppy.

(Not unique.)

3. With both the above wrong assumptions.

Lion has slit-shaped pupils,

$\therefore$ X = Great Dane, poodle or puppy.

Hyenas are related to dogs,

$\therefore$ Y = Great Dane, poodle or puppy.

X has never touched Y,

$\therefore$ Y = Great Dane, poodle or puppy.

(Not unique.)

No other wrong assumption would normally be made, so the above completes the list, and Y must be the lion.

30a

Answer

Like Fig. 4 in the question, the sides are divided into four, but in the manner shown here, giving a total of 136 pieces, and a new series, which the reader can work out.

58

Answer

B is her pocket mirror, and she is holding it in front of her face as she walks away from him, thus carrying the primary image with her. Diagram not necessary.

47

Answer

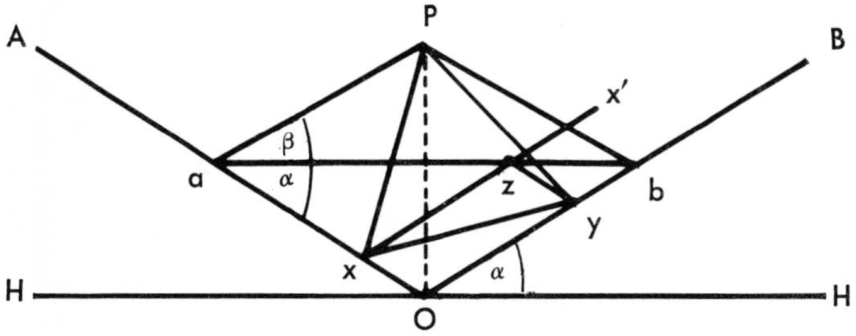

A line through OP perpendicular to the base. Again we refer to the theorem used in Puzzle 42 (and in Yaglom's book) in the version used in the photograph of the pyramids and lake. Draw AO and BO at 30° to the horizontal HH. Draw any equilateral triangle Pxy at any angle, with its lower vertices x and y on AO and BO respectively. Draw xx′ parallel to BO, and draw yz parallel to AO and intersecting xx′ at z. Draw ab through z parallel to HH. Join aP and bP.

We now regard azb as the flattened triangle—or edgewise projection—of the aforementioned theorem, and we see that, since $\alpha = 30°$, x and y are at the centroids of equilateral triangles with bases az and bz. From the theorem, regarded conversely, P must also be at the centroid of an equilateral triangle, with base ab. Therefore $\beta = 30°$. Thus in all cases P lies on PO, perpendicular to HH.

36

Answer

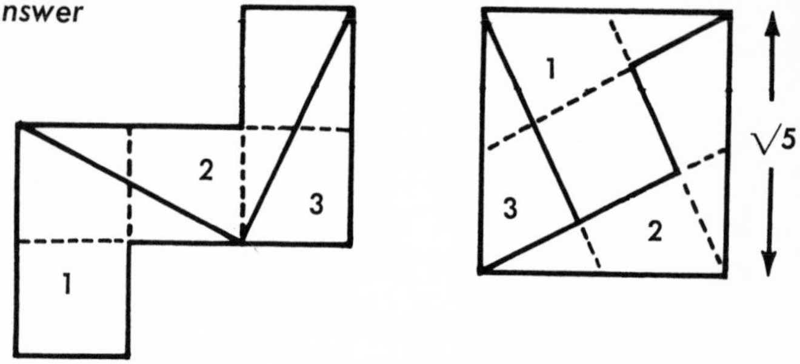

The figure shows the two cuts; the hypotenuse of Triangle $3 = \sqrt{1^2 + 2^2} = \sqrt{5}$. It will be noticed that the cut here is similar to the one in Puzzle 30.

49

Answer

63 gallons. Not 60, as it would be if measured to the level of the high-point of entry into the house, because the pipe to the basement acts as a syphon until the oil level has reached the lowest point outside the house, at D, and thus *all* the oil from the upper tank (50 gallons) and the pipe as far as D (70′ + 35′ + 25′ = 130′, or 13 gallons) is drawn in.

38

Answer

In three tries the chances of the clip remaining upright every time are *8 to 1 in favor.** Any answer equal to or better than even-money is acceptable. If the reader will try the experiment it will be found that this unexpected result is so.

Could it have been predicted? To begin with, the angle within which the clip sticks is about ⅓ of the whole circuit, Fig. 1. We shall concern ourselves with the final rotation in any one spin, as that is the one

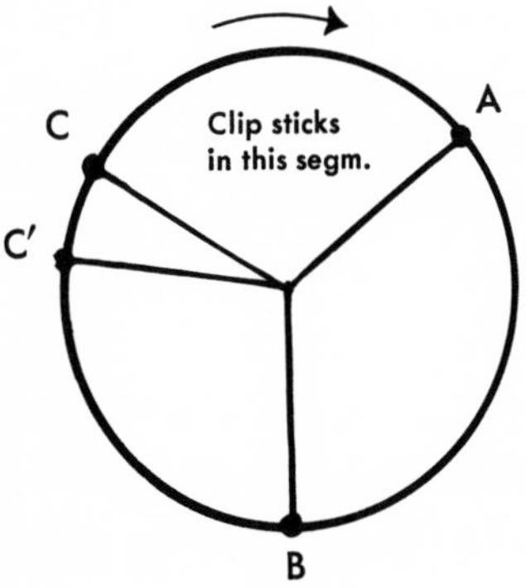

Fig. 1

* This is approximate: the writer believes it is the minimum, and in some cases the clip may go as many as 60 times without failing to stick.

when the clip stops, and it is weak enough not to be completed (we define a rotation as starting at point A). Also we rule out the segment AB, as the clip cannot stop on the way down, therefore it must stop in segment BC to fail to stick: ⅓ of the whole. But the odds can be still further reduced (of failing to stick) because once past A, the rotational momentum will be great enough at the very least to carry the clip to C′—a point close to C. Thus the angles to be compared are CA and CC′, so the chances are in our favor. Now, it is obvious that so far as *time* is concerned, the further up, the slower the clip moves: thus not only is segment CA bigger than segment CC′, but the clip will linger in the left-hand half of CA. So we can make a very rough guess at the chance being the product of 4 (by angles) and 2 (by time), so let's settle for 6, which gives a better than 50–50 chance of the sticking occurring three times in a row. In actuality, as experiment will show, it is *far greater*, in the neighborhood of 30 to 1 for a single occurrence, or 8+ to 1 for 3 in a row, and it would take great skill to flick the clip so that it did not stick.

11

Answer

1 You are ¾ my age. (This is easy on paper.)

2 Proof:

Let difference of ages be Y:

When I was X, you were $X + Y$

I am now $X + Y$, and you are $(X + Y) + Y = X + 2Y$

Twice my present age is $2(X + Y)$, or $2X + 2Y$,

$2X + 2Y$ is greater than $X + 2Y$, for all (positive) values of X and Y.

23

Answer

He reduced the 60 or 70 biggest to the size of the smallest of them, and in this way none of them stood out as isolated big ones.

31

Answer

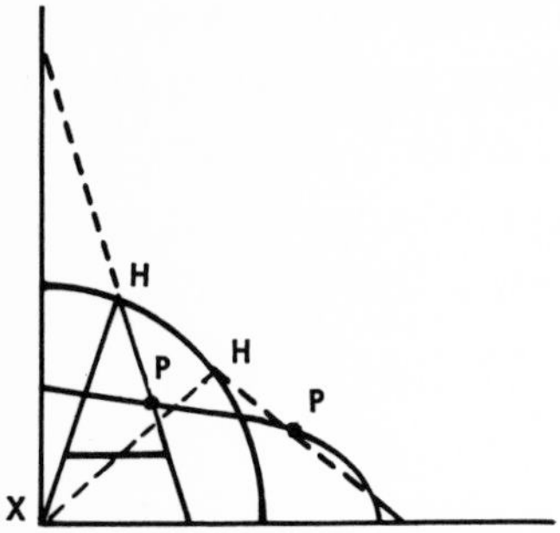

Fig. 1

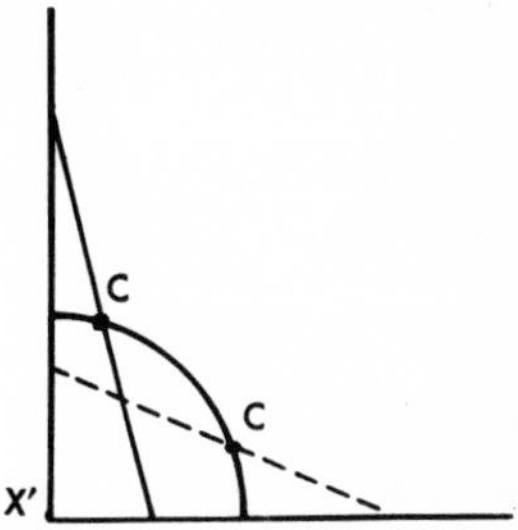

Fig. 2

A stepladder. When its crosspiece comes apart and its back legs are against an obstruction, X. The hinge H describes a quarter circle about X. If the ladder is on a smooth floor, any point P that is below H and above the bottom will describe a very exact quarter ellipse, as shown in Fig. 1.*

But one of the conditions was that the appliance not touch a wall. Since H describes a quarter circle, it forces the front part of the stepladder to move as

* We can ignore the thickness of the legs if we take P on a straight line from H to the point of contact with the floor. The fact that the feet of the ladder are not points makes very little difference.

31 Continued

though it were the lower half of a ladder twice its height (dotted) which slides down the wall. Fig. 2 shows an ordinary ladder sliding down a wall. It is well known that the center point C describes a quarter circle about X, and that any *other* point above the bottom and below the top will describe a quarter ellipse. Thus all points like P in Fig. 1 describe quarter ellipses, even when there is no wall involved.

1

Answer

There had been 16 ounces, so if B had drunk nothing the dog would have left 11 ounces, which A and B should share, getting 5½ ounces each. But A, who has drunk nothing yet, has only 5 ounces in his glass, so B should put ½ ounce back in it.

There are several other ways of working this out—some of them right.

40

Answer

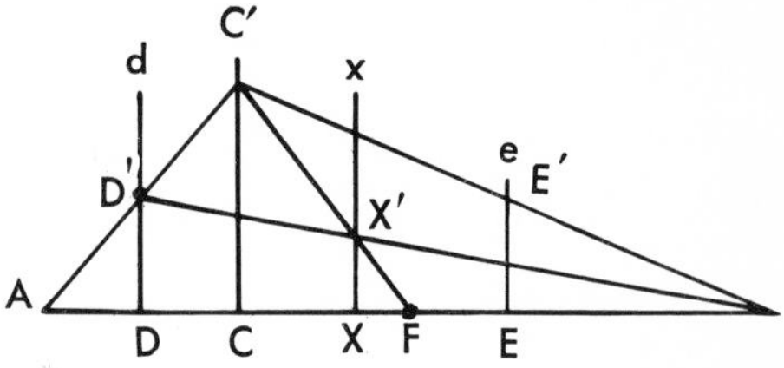

By projection, anything that is true of the relative distances of points on a straight line is also true of the projections of those points onto another straight line at any angle to the first. We imagine a triangle ABC′ to be projected onto the line AB—which can be thought of as the edgewise view of the triangle. The apex of the triangle is C′; thus D, E and F are (projections of) midpoints of the three sides. Consequently X′ is the intersection of the medians BD′ and C′F; X′ is the centroid of the triangle, and thus divides the medians into ⅓ and ⅔. Therefore BX = 2DX. The same reasoning gives AX = 2EX.

The fact that from our original diagram we only know the horizontal position of X does not affect the proof. By the parallelism of the perpendiculars Dd and Xx, the proof applies no matter what the position of X′ is on Xx: a line drawn through BX′ will always intersect Dd so that BX′ = 2D′X′. Ditto with EX. The above diagram is not necessary for the statements given in this proof.

44

Answer

The date must be 1896, 1897, 1898, or 1899 on Joan's gravestone.

For example: If Joan were born January 5, 1897 and died on her birthday, January 5, 1903, she would have died on the first day of her seventh year. The year 1900 was *not* a leap year, since it was centesimal (ending in 00), so there were no leap years during Joan's life. Thus she lived exactly six years of 365 days each, or 2190 days. If her brother John were born January 5, 1903, and died the day before his birthday, January 4, 1909 it would have only been the last day of his *sixth* year. However, during John's lifetime there would have been two leap years, 1904 and 1908. Thus, although he lived six years minus one day, two years had an extra day, making a total of 2191 days—so he lived one day longer than Joan did. For this seeming paradox to be possible, Joan can have been born no earlier than March 1, 1896, since her last year was expressed in a single digit.

25

Answer

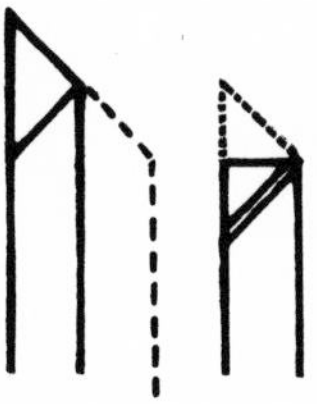

Fig. 1

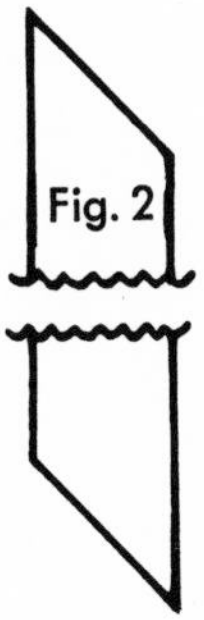

Fig. 2

He folded the belt lengthwise down the center, and then the tip down, Fig. 1.

Second Puzzle: Suppose that *both* ends were cut off at an angle of 45°, Fig. 2, what other way is possible?

Answer on page 114

29

Answer

The clue is simplicity: $\sqrt{2}$ doesn't come into it. We forget the tetrahedron for the moment, and concentrate on the four equal triangular pyramids left unoccupied by the tetrahedron: their apexes are the unlabeled corners of the cube. We take the front one, CBD, and the lowest corner. The volume of a pyramid is one-third the area of its base multiplied by its altitude. This one's base is a triangle with half the area of the base of the cube, $\frac{1}{2}$ unit, and its altitude is 1; so its volume equals $\frac{1}{6}$. There are four of these pyramids, so their total volume is $\frac{2}{3}$, leaving $\frac{1}{3}$ for the tetrahedron.

25a

Answer

Fig. 1

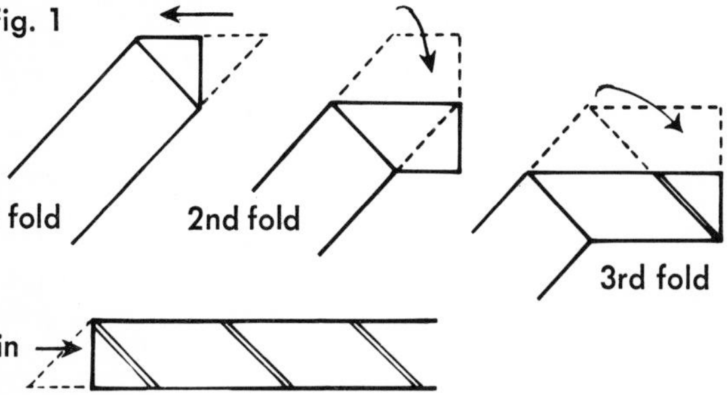

And so on until the end

If we are allowed to choose the length of the belt; then if the length is an exact multiple of its width, Fig. 1 will do it. Or if the length is a multiple of one plus four times the width: $w(4n - 1)$ where $w =$ width, and $n =$ any whole number, Fig. 2 will produce a square—which can be "rolled."

Fig. 2

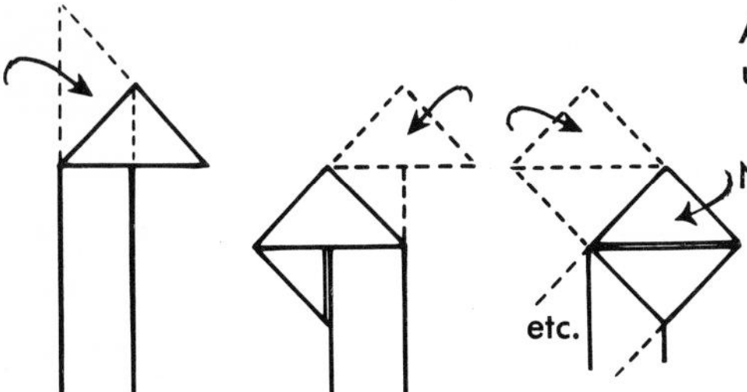

And so on until the end

1st fold 2nd fold 3rd fold

But no matter what the length might be, there is a still simpler method. What is it?

Answer on page 116

45

Answer

The cuts must run *between* the digits of the serial numbers: to reduce the spacing of cuts will lead to either joining the left half of a digit to the right half of a different one, with impossible-looking results, or if the bills are arranged so that like joins to like, there will be a duplication at the end of the series of re-arranged numbers.

The only workable strategy is to make sure that all the bills have the same number of digits per number, or if not, to rearrange them so that the group which will have the cuts between digits is taken from the beginning, or lowest numbers: because this group will, after cutting and re-joining, have one less digit per number than before, and there could be duplications. From this we can see that this group must have at least 2 digits per number; otherwise one doctored bill will have no numeral: (*Continued*)

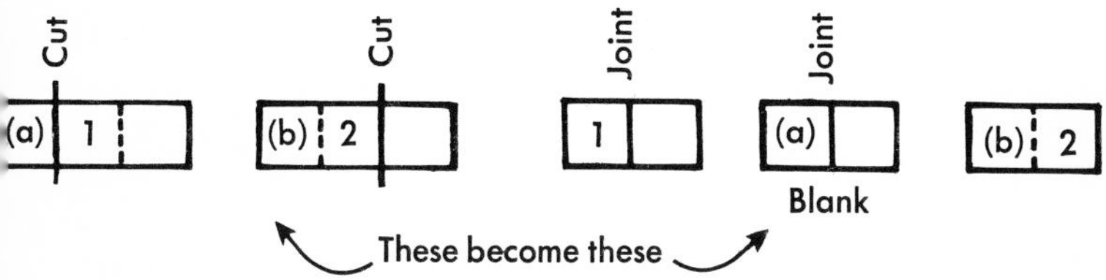

45 *Continued*

If the bills have more than 9 digits, things get complicated: the reader may care to experiment with numbered slips of paper. As to the number on the new bill, if that means the bottom or last one, its number will be that of the last of the undoctored ones. In general there will be n new numbers, and $n - 1$ original numbers lost, where $n =$ the number of digits cut between in the original bills.

25b

Answer

Bring the ends together as in the above figure.

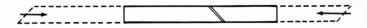

About 11½ more. We forget the volume of a man for the moment. The common knowledge needed is that the ordinary 7¼-inch milk carton holds a quart, and a quart of water weighs two pounds, and we are told that a 72-inch man weighs a little over 160 pounds. Since the box is 10 times the height of the carton, its volume is 1000 times greater, and it would hold 2000 pounds of water.

Since people and water weigh about the same—we barely float—the volume of water that the box would hold is about 2000/160 times the volume of a man; that is, the volume of the box is about 12½ times that of a man.*

* They never make fat wax dummies.

Answer

35

20

Answer

1/5 black. The "series" formed by the increasing numbers of blacks is not much help, as it merely shows how the irregular border condition gradually decreases in proportion to interior as the pattern is enlarged. Whenever the board has a multiple of five squares—25, 100, 225 etc.—the ratio is exact, and there are no alternative arrangements. The thing to notice is that every horizontal—*or* vertical, *or* diagonal—row consists of 4 white squares followed by 1 black, repeated indefinitely. At infinity the border condition can be ignored, so the total is 4 to 1: or 4/5 white and 1/5 black.

Fig. 1

(Arrows show 2 possible moves —never more than 4 sqs.)

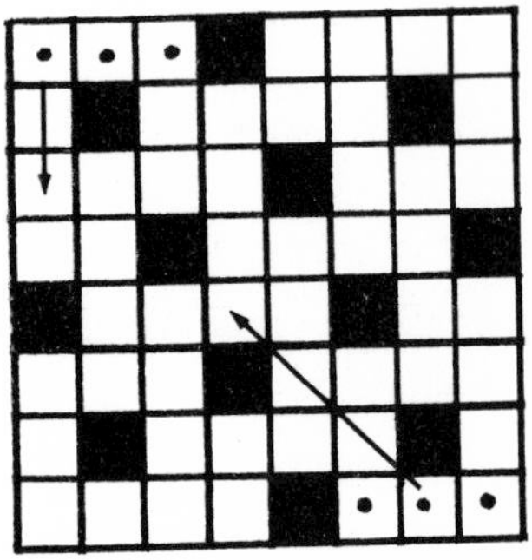

For those who like the more simple-minded board games, like Ticktacktoe, or Fox-&-Geese, a board like Fig. 1 in the question is used. There are two players, each with 3 pieces which move as chess queens, on white only. They start with the men on the dotted squares of Fig. 1, the object being to get your 3 men on the squares your opponent's men started on. No pieces are taken or jumped over. At your turn you must move or forfeit the game. Once a piece is home it remains where it is. One way of winning is to block your opponent's men so that he cannot move. It is trickier than it seems.

37

Answer

1/27. The dual of a regular tetrahedron is another regular tetrahedron, and therefore a similar figure. If we remember the following fact, the solution is easy: the centroid of a triangle divides each median so that the distance from the midpoint of a side to the centroid is 1/3 of the whole median. If the first tetrahedron has its base triangular face horizontal, its dual will be with its base face opposite and also horizontal. The altitude of the dual will therefore be 1/3 that of the original tetrahedron, and being similar, its volume will be 1/27.

39

Answer

```
  A L P H A B E T • A S T R A L
  C • A • L • • I M P • • A • A
  R A I S E D • G • P L A Y E D
  I • N • M • H E R O • S • • Y
  D E T • B A E R • S L U G • A
    D E S I G N • • I • N • I S
    G R A C E • • S T U D E N T
    E • R • • V O T E • E • D O
F A D E D • L I A R • P R I O R
A C • A • H O A R • • I • N
C H A R I O T • • B O U N D
T E • L • L • • C A E S A R
I • D I A L • P A R D • T A X
O • • E • O V A L • I • U • R
N A R R O W • I • S P A R T A
A • U • • E R N • • U • A • Y
L A N D E D • T H I S T L E S
```

7

Answer

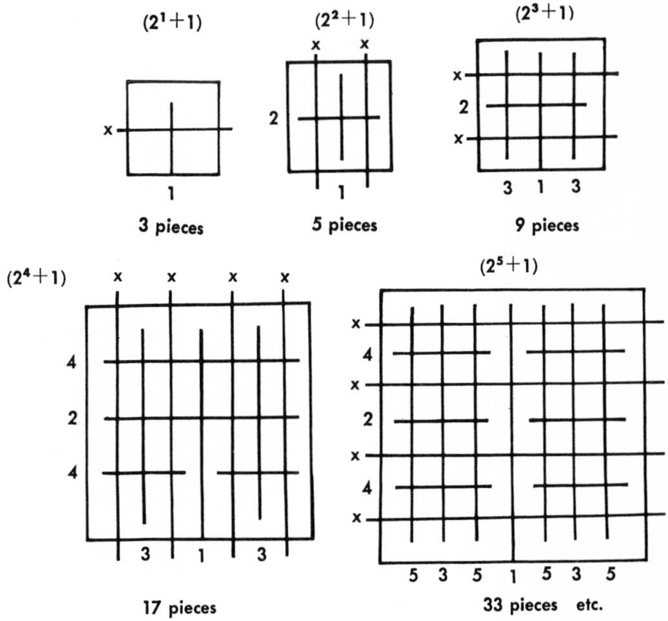

These diagrams show the result of increasing the number of cuts, the numbered ones being partial, and x being the final complete one. A few experiments with paper will show how the number increases: 3, 5, 9, 17, 33, etc. On inspection, this is seen to be the successive powers of two, plus one: $2^n + 1$, where n is the number of partial cuts. So with five partial cuts you get 33 pieces.

41

Answer

The answer:

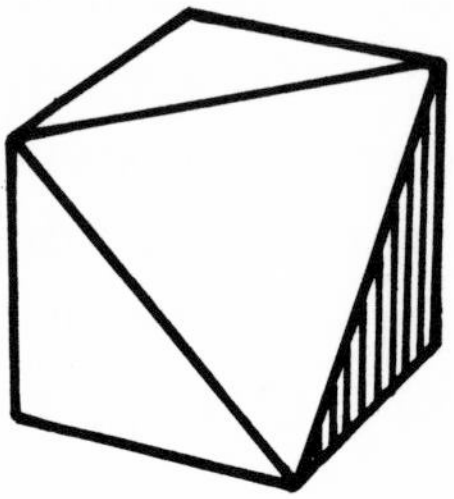

Second Puzzle: Instead of showing the three projections—front, top and right—we shall describe them, fully and accurately. All three views are as follows: a square, divided by two crossed straight lines into four equal squares.

The answers to the above are on a different page for security reasons.

Answers on page 124

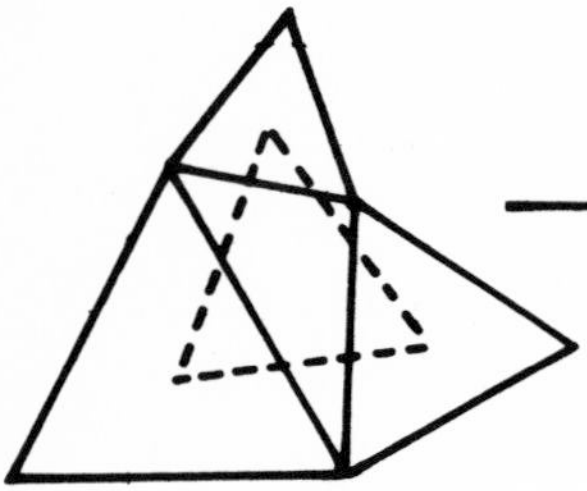

Fig. 1

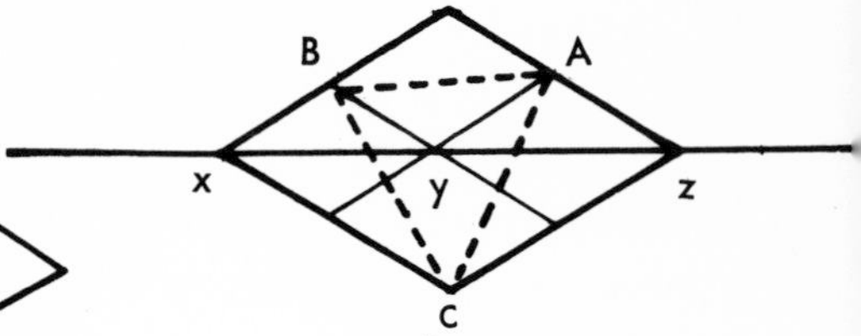

Fig. 2

There is a comparatively unfamiliar theorem recently publicized by I. H. Yaglom (*Geometric Transformations*, Random House, 1962) that is concealed in this problem. It says that if equilateral triangles are erected on the sides of *any* triangle, their centroids form another equilateral triangle, as shown in Fig. 1.

Fig. 2 shows the photograph. If we imagine the common base line of the pyramids to be the extreme (or flattened) case of a "triangle" with vertices x, y and z—or a triangle seen edgewise, as in Puzzle 40—the theorem still holds true. Since the angles of the sloping sides are 30°, the apexes are at the centroids of 3 equilateral triangles with bases xy, yz and xz. Therefore ABC is an equilateral triangle.

Answer

42

41a

Answer

Fig. 1

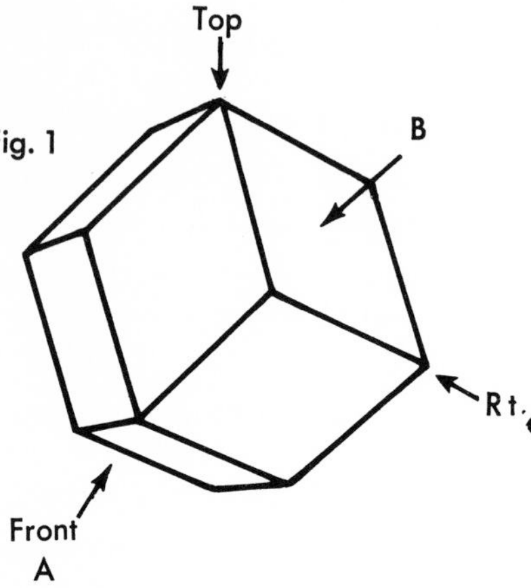

Fig. 2

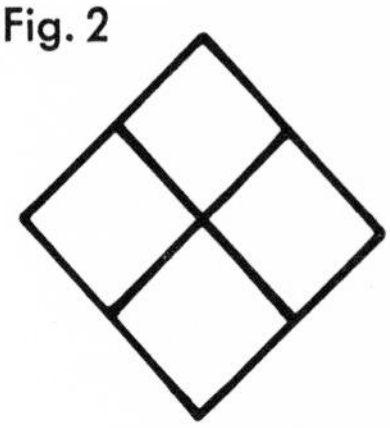

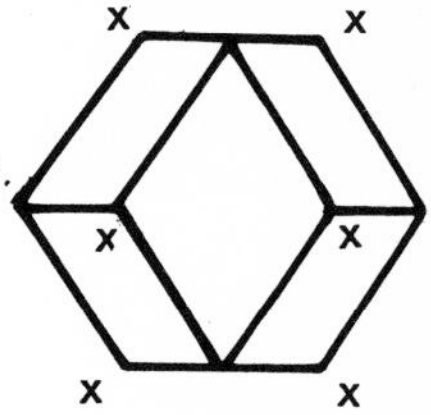

Fig. 3

Fig. 1 is a rhombic dodecahedron, balanced on one of its six four-edged vertices. The reason for describing, rather than showing, the projections is that the square in each case is tilted, Fig. 2. As Fig. 1 shows, had the square been straight it would imply that the front view was from the direction A, but the right view from B, and the projections from these viewpoints would not all be the divided squares given in the question. For example, the view from B would be Fig. 3. (The vertices marked x are three-edged.)

43

Answer

1234567890. Because the numbers in the denominator differ by 1, we can write this equivalent:

$$\frac{1234567890}{n^2 - [(n-1) \times (n+1)]}$$

Multiply:

$$\begin{array}{r} n + 1 \\ n - 1 \\ \hline -n - 1 \\ n^2 + n \\ \hline n^2 - 1 \end{array}$$

$$\therefore \text{the denominator} = n^2 - (n^2 - 1)$$
$$= 1$$

$\therefore$ the numerator is the answer. (30 seconds is enough.)

46

Answer

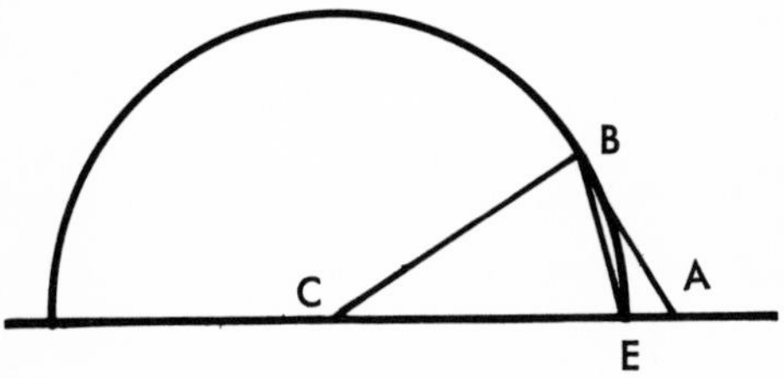

Neither. The angle ABC of the tangent at B to the center C is 90°, and since in the right-angled triangle ABC, the angle BAC is 60°, the angle ACB is 30°.

Since CE and CB are radii, the triangle EBC is isosceles, and therefore the angle BEC is 75°, and constant.

The diagram is not really necessary for these statements.

8

Answer

He heard the weather man say that a rain band was coming from the west and would arrive at New York at noon the next day. He is at X, ninety miles west of New York. He figures that as rain bands move at about thirty miles an hour it will get to X at about 9:00 A.M. He does not know where it is at broadcast time, but only that the announcer is never wrong in such estimates of time of arrival. But the rain is only going at fifteen miles an hour, so that for it to get from X to New York takes *six* hours, and therefore it passes X at 6:00 A.M.—or sooner than he expected.

34

Answer

$33\frac{1}{3}$ cups. Because there is 3% caffeine left in the doctored coffee; in 100 cups there would be enough for 3 cups of regular; 3 goes into 100 exactly $33\frac{1}{3}$ times.

52

Answer

R = S.

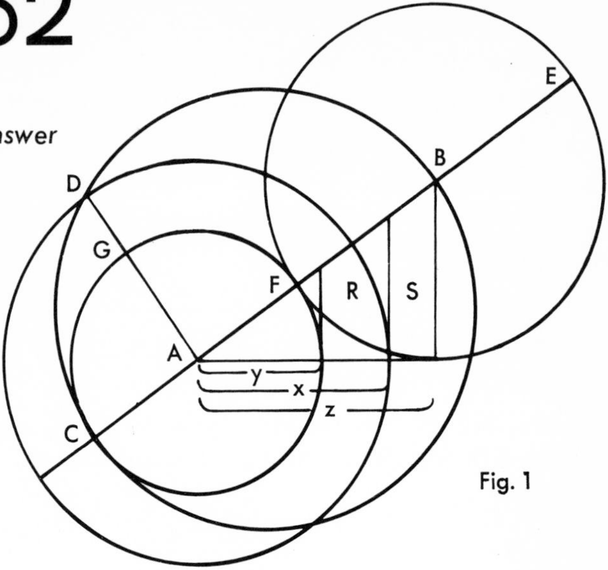

Fig. 1

The following theorems will be used:

1. Areas of similar triangles are proportional to the squares of their equivalent sides.

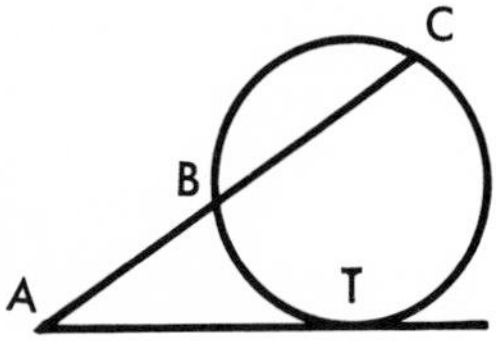

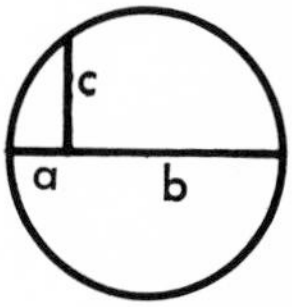

2. The area of a rectangle with sides AB and AC = $(AT)^2$, when AT is a tangent and AC is any secant to a circle.

3. The area of a rectangle with sides a and b is c^2 when a and b form a diameter of the circle and c is perpendicular to it.

Proof: In Fig. 1, $AF = AG = y$, and the area of a rectangle $AF \cdot AE = z^2$ (by Theorem 2).

Thus (also by Theorem 2) the dotted line at F divides the rectangle (as shown in Fig. 2), so that the larger part has the area $z^2 - y^2$.

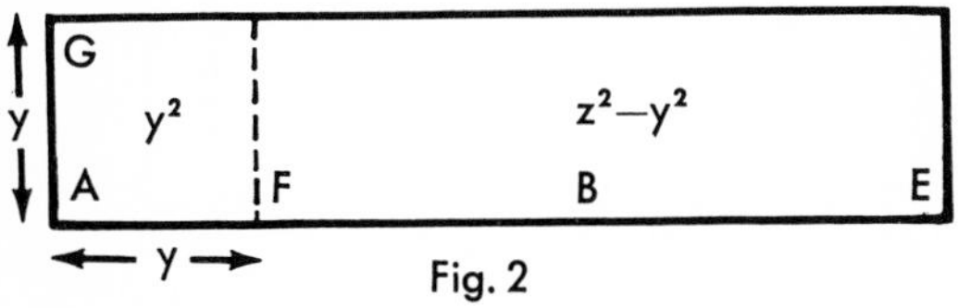

Fig. 2

Since B bisects FE, $y \cdot AB$ has the area $y^2 + \frac{z^2 - y^2}{2}$.

Then, by Theorem 3, a rectangle $CA \cdot AB$ has the area $(AD)^2$.

Since $CA = y$, a rectangle $CA \cdot AB$ = rectangle $y \cdot AB$, as mentioned above.

Also $AD = x$ (radii of the same circle).

Thus:
$$x^2 = y^2 + \frac{z^2 - y^2}{2}$$
$$x^2 - y^2 = \frac{z^2 - y^2}{2}$$
$$2x^2 - 2y^2 = z^2 - y^2$$
$$2x^2 = z^2 + y^2$$
$$x^2 - y^2 = z^2 - x^2$$

By Theorem 1, since the triangles on x, y and z are similar, $R = x^2 - y^2$ and $S = z^2 - x^2$.

Therefore the areas of R and S are equal.

A rigorous proof of the last two statements is given on page 164.

48

Answer

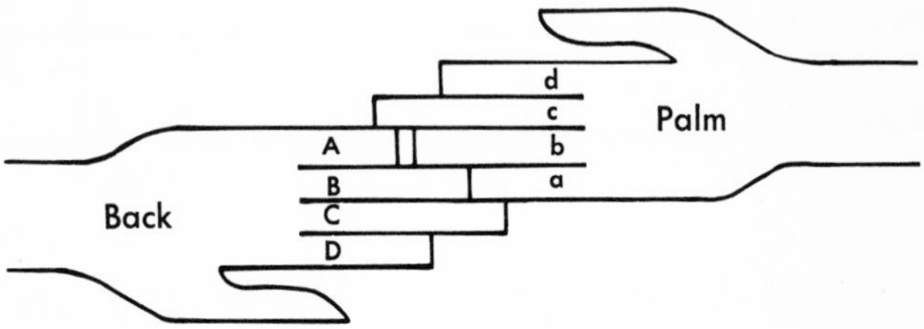

In this diagrammatic figure a method is shown that compares like to like. The sum of the little and ring fingers of the left hand is compared to the sum of ditto of the right. (The slight difference in length is exaggerated to show it; it can only be felt.) But this comparison alone proves only that $A + b < a + B$, and not which of A and b is short. The procedure is to make similar comparisons of $B + c$ with $b + C$, and $C + d$ with $c + D$. From these A can be spotted no matter what order they are made in.

If the one shown here is done first, then comparing only $B + c$ with $b + C$ is needed to identify A.

50

Answer

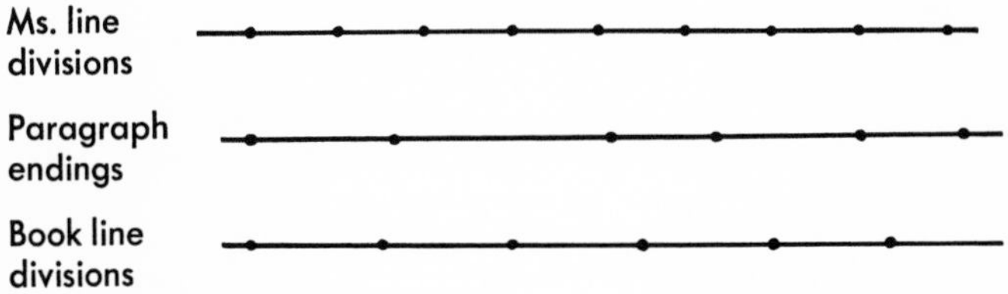

The center line shows the text printed in a single line, with paragraph endings as dots. This arrangement is fixed. The top line shows the evenly spaced line divisions of the manuscript, which, being more frequent, will have a greater chance of coinciding with the paragraph endings than will those of the book in the bottom line. The diagram is exaggerated to make it plainer.

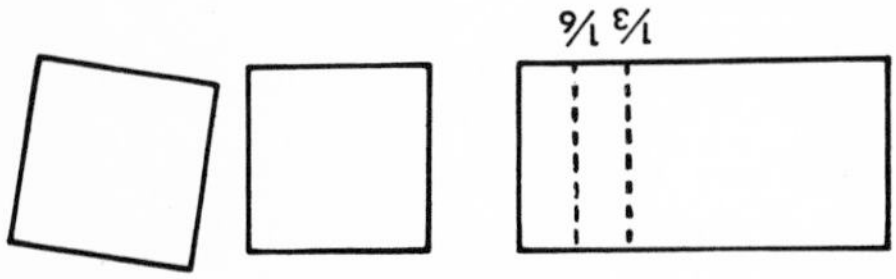

57

Answer

Two cuts, in the uncut half, at the 1/6 and 1/3 marks: the two little pieces added to the 1/4 pieces make each equal to the largest; or $1/4 + 1/12 = 4/12 = 1/3$.

53

Answer

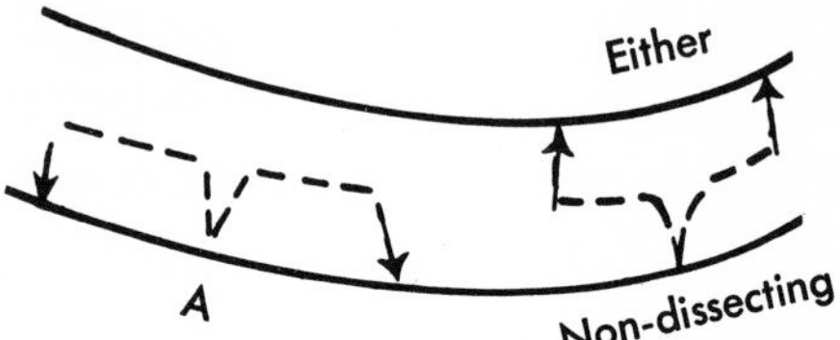

Fig. 1

At any point, depending on how the cross-cut reaches it. The one-sidedness of a Moebius strip is not quite as simple as it sounds: Its single side can be looked at from two directions, just as a geometrical line with numbered points can be. If these numbers ran from left to right, seen from the opposite direction they would run from right to left. In Fig. 1, part of a Moebius strip, when the cut leaves A, to dissect the strip, if it turns to the left it must turn to the left *again* to meet the edge, or vice versa. Put more generally: it must turn twice in the same sense *as seen from the same direction.* That direction will have reversed itself when we come back to where we started. The non-dissecting cut must go first left and then right, or vice versa. The length of the cut has no effect on this rule. In Fig. 2, if we follow the cut with our eye we see that the direction of view—by which we judge left-or-right—has changed from –1– to –2–, and a right turn from that direction will take the cut to B, dissecting the strip. A *left* turn here would take the cut to C, or even to its own beginning at A, or itself, and any of these would leave the strip in one piece—a long unjoined band.

(*Continued*)

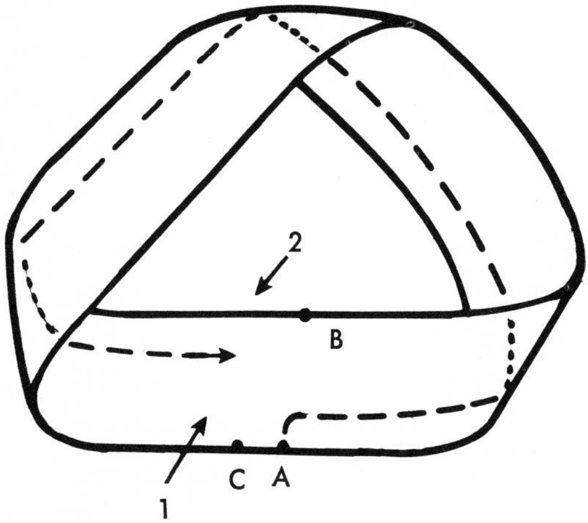

Fig. 2

53 *Continued*

Puzzle 2: The above rule tacitly assumes the cut to be in three straight segments. Give a more general rule that would allow the cut to be any curve that does not meet or cross itself.

Answer on page 136

51

Answer

14765636901636567490 . . . repeated ad inf. The series does not repeat after the 10th term as one might think, but after the 20th. We write down the ten digits on the top line:

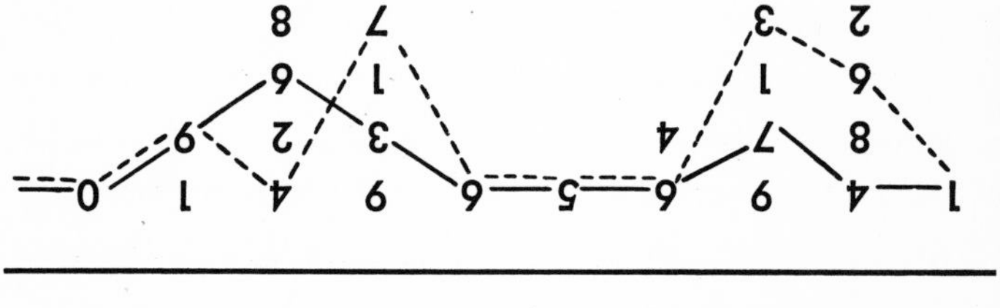

Under each we write the last digit of the result of squaring the digit above; e.g., $8 \times 8 = (6)4$. Then we multiply each digit in the 2nd line by the digit in the top line, and if it differs from the digit in the second line, we put down the last digit of the result; e.g., $3 \times 9 = (2)7$, but under 1, 5, 6 and 0 (top line) we leave a blank, as they keep repeating. The process is carried on with each until a cyclic repeat is formed: the longest being four, for 2, 3, 7 and 8. By counting we now find in each column the terminal digits of the succeeding powers in question: thus with the case of 7, 9 is for the second power: $7 \times 7 = (4)9$, 3 for the 3rd, 1 for the 4th, 7 for the 5th (the repeat), then back to 9 for the 6th, and 3 for the 7th, the one we want. But we keep going in this way, and at the 17th we get 7. Carrying on the process—quite easy to do in the head—we find that the 27th power brings us back to 3, and from then on it is obvious that the occurrence of these will be every 10th position; 3 and 7 will alternate. The same holds for the columns under 2, 3 and 8, while with 4 and 9, 6 and 9 respectively will always occur. The solid lines indicate the path of the first time around, and the dotted lines the second. From then on the routes alternate, giving the series shown at the beginning.

53a

Answer

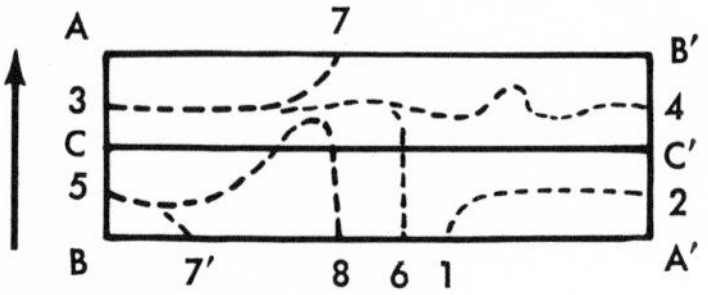

Fig. 1

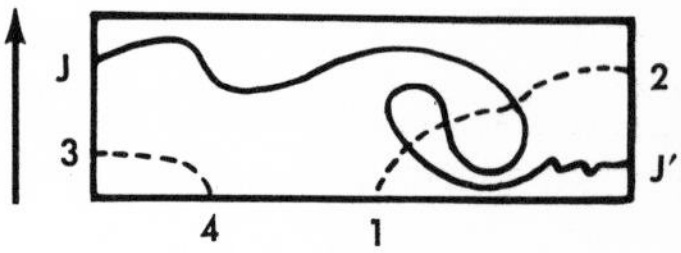

Fig. 2

Fig. 1 is a convenient way to show a Moebius strip, shortened and unjoined, but showing how the joint should go, by means of the vertical arrows, which mean that the *ends only* are joined, and that A joins to A′, and B to B′; or with a half twist. Thus a cut (dotted) starting at 1 and going to 2 would, because of the twist, reappear at 3, etc. One might think that provided a crosscut starting at 1 and ending at 6 *does* cross over the center line, CC′, the strip is *not* dissected; but that if the cut *does not* cross the line—branching instead to 7 or 7′—then the strip *is* dissected.

Unfortunately, if the cut takes the route ending at 8, the rule no longer holds. Furthermore, why a straight center line?

In topology it is sometimes convenient in cases like this to refer to a Jordan curve: a "simple" loop, i.e., that neither touches nor crosses itself, and divides the surface it is on into two distinct areas, provided that surface is like this page, without holes or unusual joints. The correct and most general rule, to replace the one above, is that if any simple curve, JJ′, Fig. 2, is drawn—on both sides at once, like a cut—so that it begins at one end of the diagram and ends where it joins its starting point when the strip is twisted and joined, thus making a Jordan curve that makes *one circuit only*, then any cross-cut that crosses it an *odd number of times will not dissect the strip*. Conversely, *no* crossings, or an *even number* of them, *will* dissect the strip.

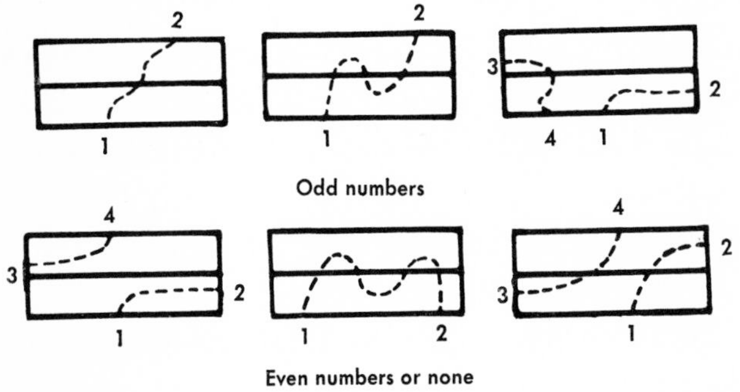

Fig. 3

Fig. 3 shows some examples of both, with the Jordan curve made arbitrarily straight for clarity, but it can be any shape provided it does not quite touch the edge; like Fig. 2. *(Continued)*

53a *Continued*

Note: It is not the number of wiggles in the cut that matter, merely the number of crossings of the Jordan curve once it has been established. The proof involves the proof of the Jordan curve theorem, and set theory, both too complicated to go into here. It does, however, show that although the edge of a Moebius strip is indeed one single edge, there is a real, though movable and imaginary, line which divides the edge from itself in certain contexts. A very loose analogy would be to say that if you sail from New York harbor, make an odd number of crossings of the Atlantic, and end up in New York harbor, you must have circumnavigated the world and returned via the Panama Canal (or the Horn) and sailed up the coast. Or you went into orbit.

60

Answer

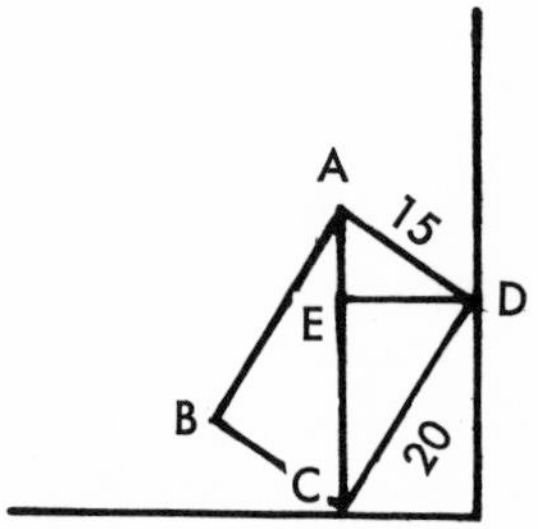

12 inches. The expert may be in trouble if he gets the equation to the curve, and then places H by calculus, but if we remember that the high point is reached by A when the diagonal AC is vertical, all we need is the perpendicular distance of D from the hypotenuse of the right triangle ACD. The hypotenuse AC is 25 inches, since the proportion of the other two sides is as 3 to 4. And since the distance DE is to AD as AB is to AC, we get

$$\frac{DE}{15} = \frac{20}{25} \quad \text{or } DE = \frac{15 \times 20}{25} = 12$$

54

Answer

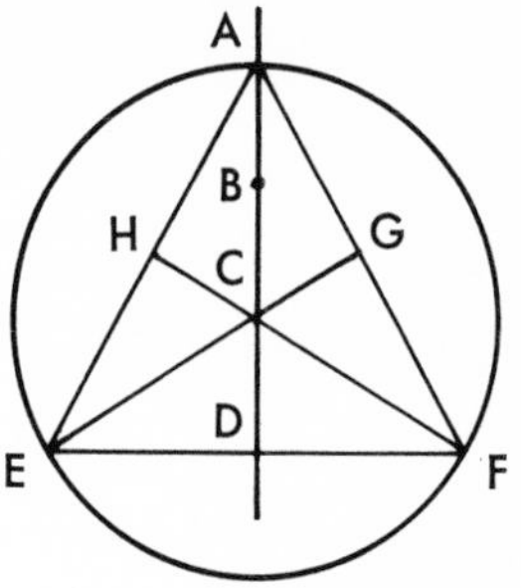

He made use of the theorem that the centroid of a triangle divides a median at the one-third point. He had drawn a vertical line, and with the marking strip laid off 3 contiguous equal lengths on it: AB, BC, and CD. Then, with C as center, he had drawn a nearly complete circle through A, and EDF perpendicular to AD, cutting the arc at E and F. He joined AE and AF: EAF was the equilateral triangle.

Proof:

Draw ECG and FCH.

Since AD is part of the diameter, DE = DF; also AC = 2CD.

Therefore C is the centroid, and the three lines through it are medians, each of which is 1½ a radius.

Thus they are equal, and the triangle is equilateral. Q.E.D.

Puzzle 2: What would the man have done if he had not known the centroid theorem—or square roots?

Answer on page 142

55

Answer

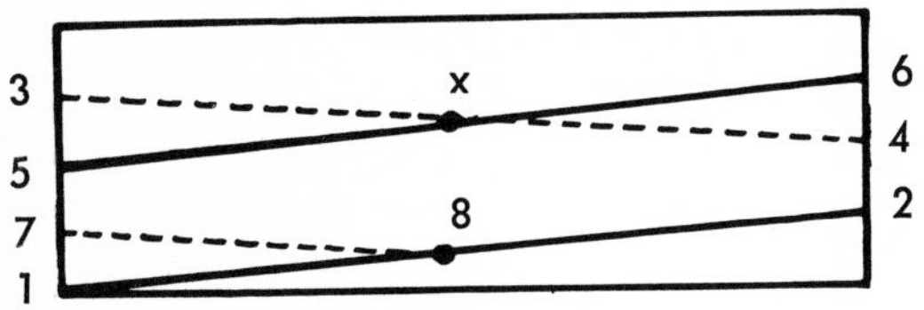

When joined, 2 meets 3, 4 meets 5, and 6 meets 7.

Also direction of slant changes.

Fig. 1

Before joining the strip mark it off as in Fig. 1, which is here shortened. The numbered points are at the half and quarter positions, and the line is ruled on the back where dotted. When joined, the line will be straight and continuous. The cut starts at 1 and proceeds numerically; after 5, when x is reached, the strip opens out, so the cut must continue on the rest of the line. It thus seems not to be continuous, but the *line was*.

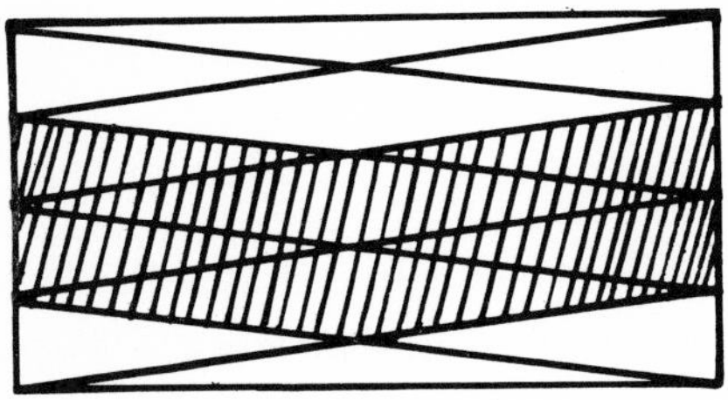

Fig. 2

When point 8 is reached the strip comes apart into two pieces of equal area, which is proved by counting the triangles in Fig. 2. The shaded part is one piece and the unshaded part the other; each contains eight triangles of equal area (a quarter of a rectangle).

54a

Answer

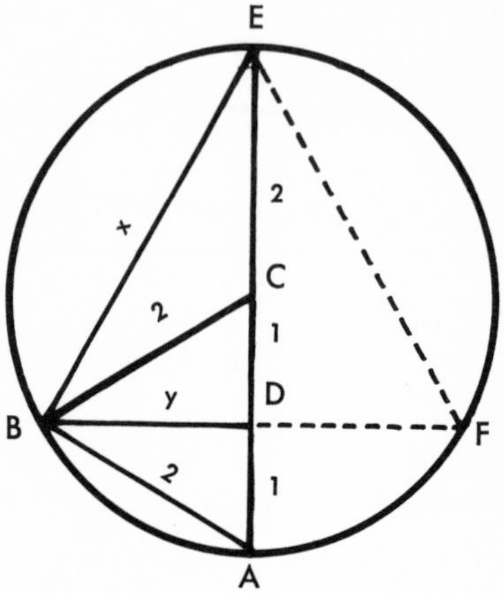

Circle completed, relabeled

The same as before.

Proof:

Since BD is perpendicular to AC, and AD = CD, triangle ABC is isosceles.

Therefore AB = 2.

Since it is in a semicircle, ∠ ABE = 90°, and

Since ∠ BAE is common to △ ABD and △ ABE, they are similar.

The hypotenuse AE of △ ABE = 4; the hypotenuse AB of △ ABD = 2.

Therefore x = 2y.

And x = BF = FE.

Q.E.D.

56

Answer

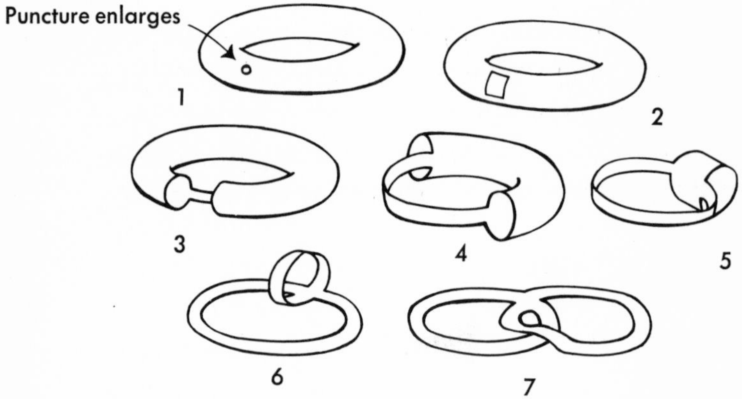

The minimum number of colors is seven. Naturally, the small oblong and round inlays are ignored: being islands, they merely differ from their common backgrounds. Topologists will recognize the paths as the equivalent—or homeomorph—of a torus (punctured). The latter is the surface of a wedding ring or bagel, and it has been proved that it can be so subdivided that the resultant map may need as many as seven colors, but never more; which is odd, considering that the four-color problem for simple surfaces, e.g., any map on a globe, has not been proved. The figure here shows how a punctured torus (the puncture does not affect the necessity of seven colors) is gradually distorted into the Hokusai pathways. There are other map designs on a torus that need seven colors.

61

Answer

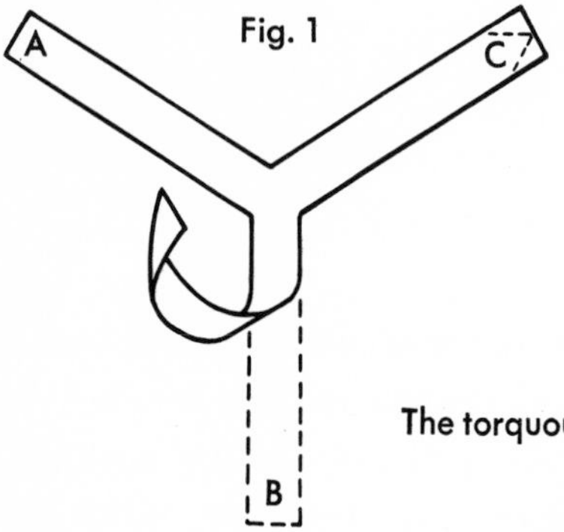

Fig. 1

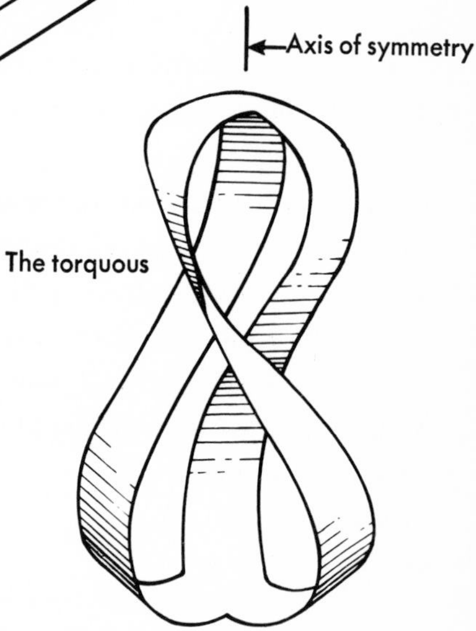

Fig. 2

Fig. 1 shows how B has been given a half twist, counterclockwise, and bent up. The same is then done to A and C, and the three are joined, which will be easier to do if C, say, is cut to a 60° point. It will be seen that there are two sides and one edge, corresponding to the single edge of the puncture; therefore it has one hole. If any two of the three arms are cut across, the model remains in one piece, satisfying the Betti number of 2. Fig. 2 shows the final form: it is called a *torquous,* for obvious reasons.

Puzzle 2 (for topologists): In what respect does the torquous differ from a torus?

Puzzle 3: Fig. 3 shows a map that needs seven colors when on a torus: it is flattened out here, and was the one distorted to fit on the paths of Hokusai's garden, Puzzle 56. Now make it fit on the torquous. When the top and bottom edges are joined, the ends of the resultant tube are joined. The puncture is then one, and does not affect the map.

Answers on page 149

This edge bent back, joined to bottom.

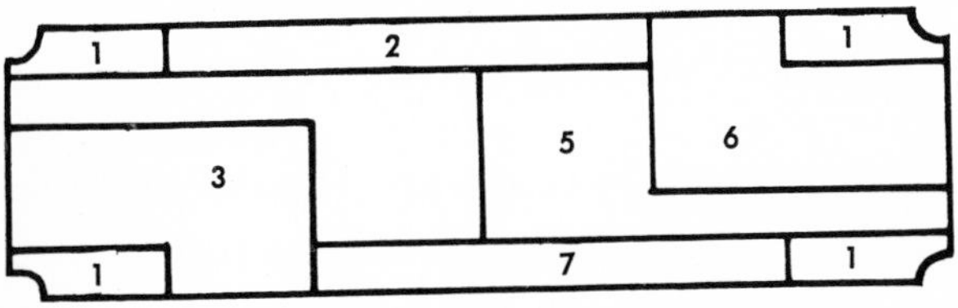

One of 4 quarters of puncture

One of 4 quarters of area 1

Fig. 3

59

Answer

Yes, in two cuts. The clue is that if "distinguished mathematicians" have proved that 6 cuts are necessary, there is probably nothing wrong with their math. The only thing left, since the problem is being posed again in the face of the given proofs, is to re-examine the wording of the question.

Once, when a distinguished scientist was asked how a man of Sir Oliver Lodge's eminence could be bamboozled by the trickery of fraudulent spiritualists, he replied that at a conjuring show it is well to watch the conjurer's other hand, but in lab work scientists don't look suspiciously under the bench. It is probable that the above mathematicians took the intention for the word: for example, to rearrange the pieces "after each cut" obviously does not mean "after *every* cut," as it would be pointless after the last one. And once that is admitted, we can say, "after some cut or cuts," and the problem is then solved by saying we shall rearrange after the first cut and during the second: nothing was said to preclude it, and no limit was imposed on the number of pieces cut through in "one cut."

No rearrangement is possible until after the first cut

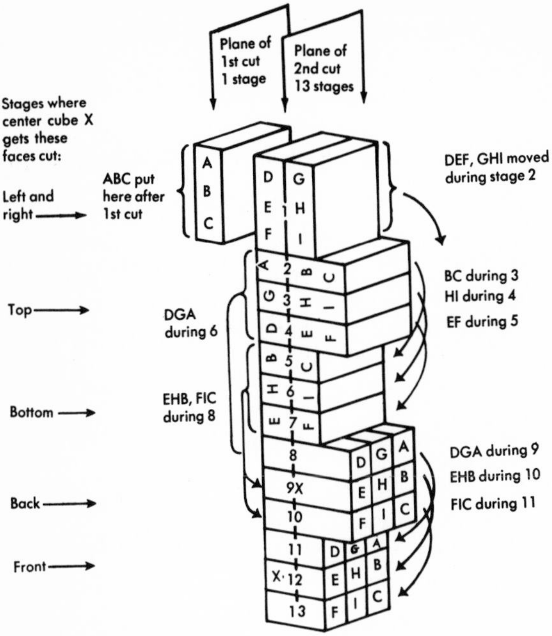

(Finish)

is finished, since the block is still in one piece, but the second cut goes through 13 separate layers—one of them triple thickness. No special jig is needed to hold the work: it rests on the cutting surface and is slid along the saw horizontally, and kept in alignment by a metal guide at the back. The figure shows the program of replacing the detached pieces during the second cut: try to work it out before looking—13 *layers.*

The sequential arrangement is here shown as a vertical assembly; the saw cut is vertical and the lettered sur-

59 *Continued*

face of the original cube which faces us here would, in practice, be its bottom which rests on the cutting table. The metal guide would be to the left of what we see here. As pieces become detached behind the saw (above, in this diagram) they are removed and put at the other end (below, here) and the pressure of the column is continued against the saw. We show all the rearrangements at once, giving the procedure at the side. The six places where the center 1-inch cube gets its six necessary cuts are shown in the left column.

61a

Answer

Puzzle 2:

The edge is tied in a trefoil knot, which cannot be traced on a torus. The H_1 (homology group) differs from that of a torus.

Puzzle 3:

To attempt to make the distortion in one step leads to headaches; we must make a sneak attack on the problem, and first distort the torquous, using the Hokusai pathways as a guide. The main difference between the latter and the torquous is that the torquous has two junctures with three elements meeting at each, and the other has one juncture with four meeting at it. Fig. 1

61a *Continued*

Fig. 1

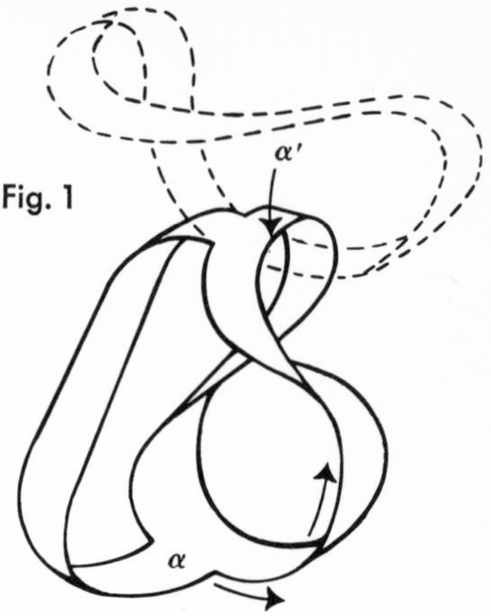

Fig. 2

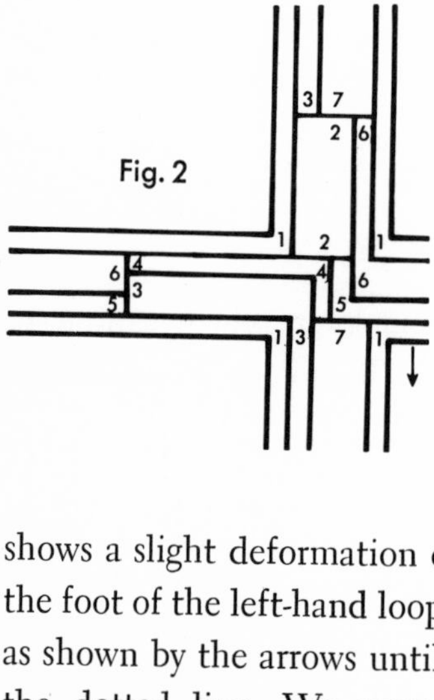

Fig. 3

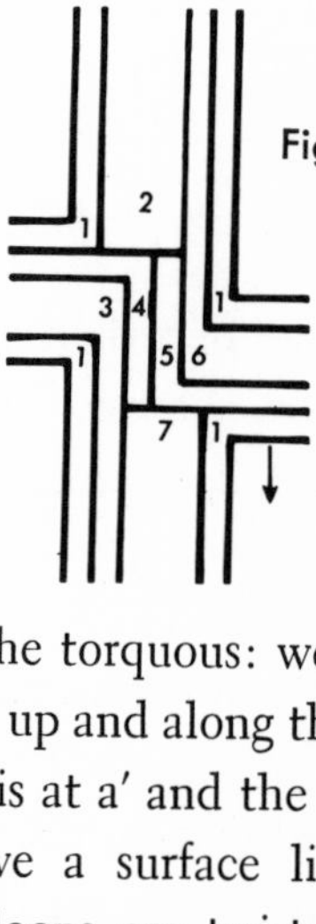

shows a slight deformation of the torquous: we move the foot of the left-hand loop, a, up and along the edge as shown by the arrows until it is at a′ and the loop is the dotted line. We now have a surface like the Hokusai pathways except the loops are twisted, but since they are double twists, and thus retain their two-sidedness, we can ignore the twists in mapmaking. Fig. 2 shows the new quadruple juncture with the map on it as on Hokusai's pathways. Figs. 3 and 4 show how the nexus of the map elongates as we move a back to where it belongs, and Fig. 5 shows how the two restored triple junctures look when made equiangular on a modified model for the torquous: A is given a half twist which, when they are brought up, places C over C′, and B over B′, ready to be given their half twists and joined, B to B′ and C to C′.

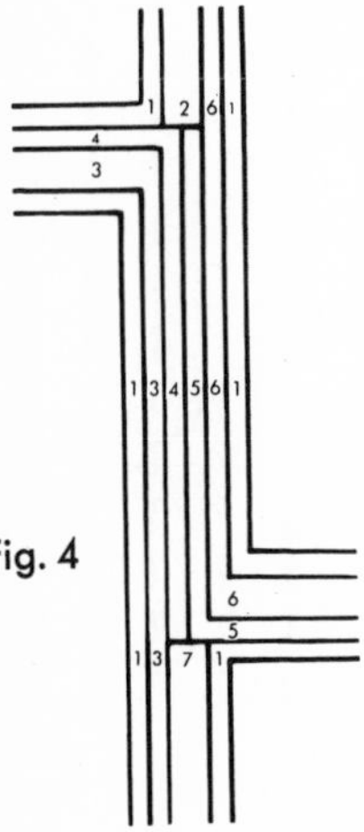

Fig. 4

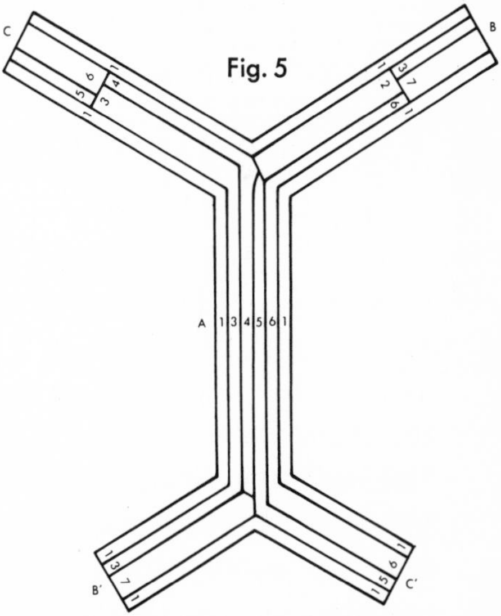

Fig. 5

62

Answer

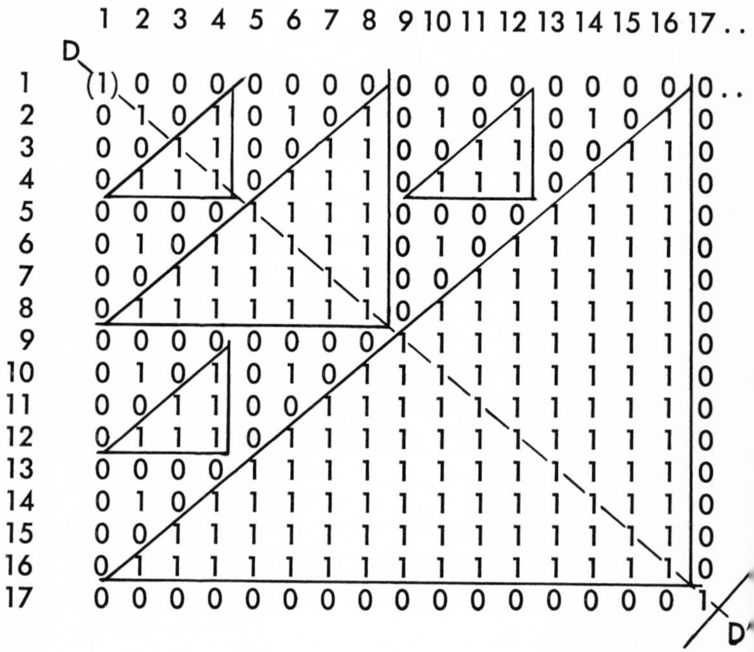

The pattern never repeats as a complete square of any finite size. The triangles of 1's running down the diagonal DD′ almost double in size every time—their bases measure one less than the successive powers of 2:

(1), 3, 7, 15, 31 . . . etc. The other fact the reader will have noticed is that the pattern as a whole is symmetrical about DD′. It is this symmetry that shows why the pattern will never repeat as a finite square.

"Rows" means the horizontals, and "columns" means the verticals, and a given symbol is indicated thus; 5,3 means the fifth on the third row—or five across and three down. Say we have put down the first four rows and columns. When we put down the fifth row we are back with four 0's, and the same with the fifth column, but owing to symmetry, symbol 5,5 will be a 1, and for the same reason at the lower right-hand corner of each succeeding triangle on DD′ there will always be a 1 in the next place in the row below—thus making the diagonal DD′ a series of 1's, so that we can never get a repeat of the first row or column (0's forever).

Question 2: Can a repeating pattern be made by starting differently? *

Answer on page 154

* Excluding the dull one; 1's all over.

62a

Answer

(In the figures the 1 at the beginning is assumed if we count the repeating series back.)

Fig. 1

	1	2	3	4	5	6	7	
1	1	0	0	1	0	0	1	. . .
2	0	1	0	0	1	0	0	
3	0	0	1	0	0	1	0	
4	1	0	0	1	0	0	1	
5	0	1	0	0	1	0	0	
6	0	0	1	0	0	1	0	
7	1	0	0	1	0	0	1	

D ... D′

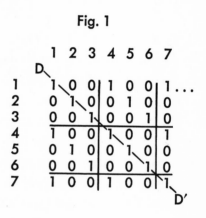

By blind experiment or luck we might discover that a row, and column, of a 1 and two o's repeated gives the endlessly repeating pattern of Fig. 1: a 3 × 3 square. If we analyze what caused the nonrepeating but enlarging pattern given by o's alone, we must stop to think why an arrangement—any arrangement—of symbols along the first row and the *same* down the first column will give symmetry about the diagonal DD′.

Fig 2

D

	1	2	3
1		X	X
2	X	1	X
3	X	X	1

D′

Fig. 3

D

	1	2	3	4
1	(1)	0	0	1
2	0	1	0	0
3	0	0	1	0
4	1	0	0	1

D′

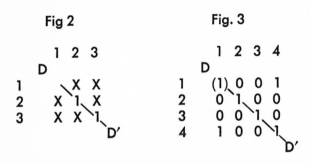

In Fig. 2 we take the symbols, given as X's, at 2,1 and 1,2: by our rule they are the same, so symbol 2,2 will be a 1 whatever X stands for. Also, since 3,1 and 1,3 are the same symbol they will either both agree or both disagree with the symbol to which we compare them. Therefore 3,2 and 2,3 will be alike, and 3,3 will be a 1. This continues to happen, so that row *n* and column *n* will always be alike, and where they cross—on the diagonal DD′—there will always be a 1. In the case of Fig. 1, what happens is that the presence of 1's at 4,1 and 1,4 prevents the formation of three 1's in row 4 and column 4, and we get instead *an exact repeat* of row 1 and column 1. (*Continued*)

62a *Continued*

Fig. 4

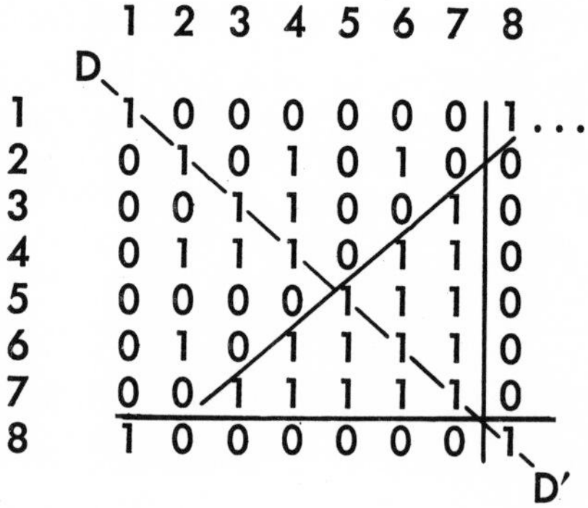

Consider the triangle of 1's with base at row 8 in the diagram on page 152. Fig. 4 shows it taken to row 7, column 7. In the diagram's original form the next 0 in column 1 gave the bottom row of 1's, which were then changed to 0's *by the next 0 in column 1*. We now instead put a 1 at row 8, column 1: the result of this is to make the inevitable 1 on diagonal DD′ match the 1 we have put in our altered series—the same 1 being also put at row 1, column 8—and the new row and column 8 are exact repeats of row 1 and column 1, and the pattern, a 7×7 square, will repeat indefinitely. The same maneuver can be done, instead, at the base of any other of the triangles on DD′, merely giving larger repeat squares. From this we derive the formula that any starting series that consists of 1 followed by $2^n - 2$ zeros will repeat.

Question 3: What other repeating patterns can be got by the method given above, but not according to the given formula ($2^n - 2$)?
Answer on page 158

62b

Answer

	1	2	3	4	5	6	7	8
1	1	0	0	0	0	0	0	1 . . .
2	0	1	0	1	0	1	0	0
3	0	0	1	1	0	0	1	0
4	0	1	1	1	0	1	1	0
5	0	0	0	0	1	1	1	0
6	0	1	0	1	1	1	1	0
7	0	0	1	1	1	1	1	0
8	1	0	0	0	0	0	0	1

D — D′

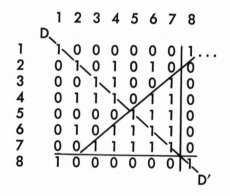

Apart from the series that conform to the formula 1000 . . . $2^n - 2$ zeros, every series formed by a row (or column) within a repeating square will recreate the same repeating pattern, provided we start at the diagonal DD′. For example, the figure here shows the pattern given on page 156; if we take row 2, and start with the 1 at 2,2, we get a series, 1 0 1 0 1 0 0, repeated, and it, with a similar column, will obviously recreate the same over-all pattern, merely stripped of its first row and column.

The same thing happens with the other five series in this square: e.g., the one on row 6, starting at the diagonal DD′ and moving cyclically, is 1 1 0 1 0 1 1, repeated. In the next bigger triangle, with base on row 15 (made to repeat), we get another, bigger set of internal series, and so on *ad infinitum*.

We shall not go into the subject of asymmetrical patterns: the reader can experiment with them—they are quite irritating. E.g., with row 1 being 1 0 repeating, and column 1 being 1 0 0 repeating, the pattern becomes asymmetrical in the first 3 × 3 square. *Warning:* just *one* error wrecks the rest of the pattern—uncorrectably.

Question 4: If we call the method we have been using "deductive," what can be done inductively? In particular, what can be learned about the enlarging nonrepeating pattern on page 152 *by induction?*
Answer on page 160

62c

Answer

	−3	−2	−1	1	2	3
−3	1	1	1	0	1	0
−2	1	1	1	0	0	1
−1	1	1	1	0	1	1
1	1	1	1	0	0	0
2	1	1	1	0	1	0
3	1	1	1	0	0	1

Fig. 1

"Inductive" in this case means working backward, and the rule becomes this: The symbol *over* a 1 is the same as the symbol to the left of the 1, and the symbol *over* a 0 is different from the symbol to the left of the 0. According to this, a row of 0's would give a row of 1's over it, but if we want to have row 1 and column 1 continue back and up with the same 0's, we are constrained to put a 1 in the 1,1 position—otherwise it contradicts the facts. Fig. 1 shows what happens if we continue column 1 upward, with a 1 in the 1,1 position—we get nothing to the left but a solid bank of 1's, and cannot put 0's along row 1 to the left. Fig. 2 shows what we get with the proper arrangement: it is obvious that at 3, −1 we get a row of 1's continuing forever. Then on row −2, one step to the right, another infinite row of 1's starts, and we see the beginning of an infinite triangle of 1's. The same thing happens in the lower left

D

	−6	−5	−4	−3	−2	−1	1	2	3	4	5	6	7	8
−6	1	1	1	1	1	1	0	1	0	1	0	1	0	1
−5	1	1	1	1	1	1	0	0	1	1	0	0	1	1
−4	1	1	1	1	1	1	0	1	1	1	0	1	1	1
−3	1	1	1	1	1	1	0	0	0	0	1	1	1	1
−2	1	1	1	1	1	1	0	1	0	1	1	1	1	1
−1	1	1	1	1	1	1	0	0	1	1	1	1	1	1 . . .
1	0	0	0	0	0	0	1	0	0	0	0	0	0	0 . . .
2	1	0	1	0	1	0	0	1	0	1	0	1	0	1 . . .
3	0	1	1	0	0	1	0	0	1	1	0	0	1	1
4	1	1	1	0	1	1	0	1	1	1	0	1	1	1
5	0	0	0	1	1	1	0	0	0	0	1	1	1	1
6	1	0	1	1	1	1	0	1	0	1	1	1	1	1

D′

Fig 2

quadrant, and we seem to be getting a rather unorthodox view of the three corners of the final (at infinity) triangle our original pattern was aiming at, the upper left quadrant showing its bottom right corner: all 1's.

Question 5

Hint (for lower mathematicians): Going back to our original pattern (page 152), what is the ratio of 1's to the whole when the pattern is carried to infinity? We can see a series starting: in the first, 2×2, square there are 2 out of 4; in the 4×4 square, 8 out of 16, then 38 in 64, then 176 in 256, etc. Such a series is rather forbidding, so, can we determine the proportion of the *area* taken up by the 1's, by a sort of geometrical model?

Answer on page 162

62d

Answer

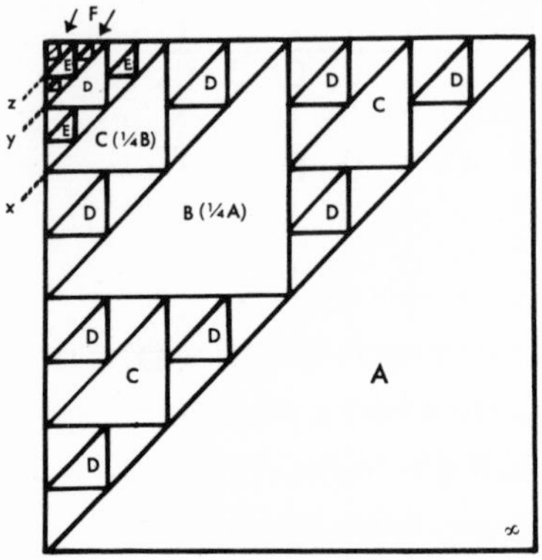

Fig. 1

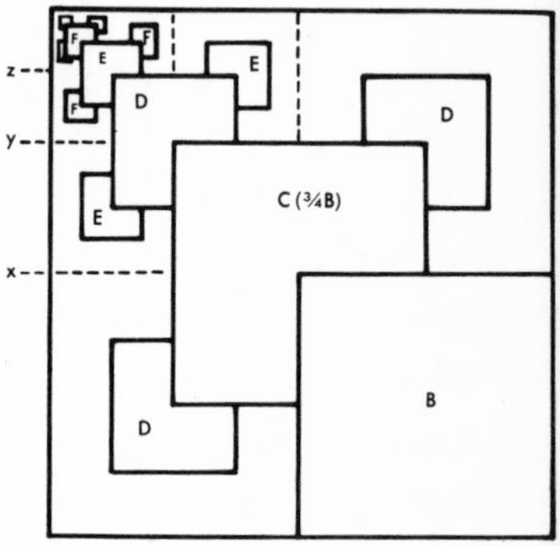

Fig. 2

100%.

We ignore series for the moment, and draw the pattern as though seen through the wrong end of a telescope, regarding infinity as a *fait accompli*. In Fig. 1, A is the final triangle at infinity, and B the next one in, etc., and we imagine that the pattern is filled in, in the way it was previously filled out—we here show more and more in the upper left corner. Fig. 2 shows a geometrical analogy of this, but with the areas doubled and made square: A, shown incompletely at the right, is the correspondent of the big triangle A in Fig. 1; B, in Fig. 2, is 1/4 the size of A; etc. It will be seen that the subsequent squares—we do not in this case need to keep filling them all in—conform to this proportionate rule: the 3 D's in Fig. 2 being proportional to the 9 D's in Fig. 1.

It takes no very great mathematical sagacity to realize that the series 1, 1/2, 1/4, 1/8 . . . adds up to 2, if we think of ourselves standing two paces away from a wall; taking one pace toward the wall; then half a pace, then a quarter, and so on—always half the remaining distance—an infinite number of times. It is obvious that this Achillean approach will take us a total of two paces. This, we can see, applies to the way in which the ever-decreasing squares in Fig. 2 approach the confines of their containing squares, marked with dotted lines, x, y, z, etc. At infinity the whole space is filled by the lettered squares, and so in Fig. 1 it is filled by the triangles of 1's.

While it is true that there is an infinity of 0's, the ratio as expressed by the areas occupied by 1's and 0's is as a square to its side: the *whole* area is taken up by the square. If any higher mathematician cavils at this, remind him of puzzle 20, and if he still complains, mention Cantor sets, and leave the room.

R.I.P.

Additional Argument for Answer 52

Since the triangles on x, y and z are similar, we have, from Theorem 1,

$$K : K + R : K + R + S = y^2 : x^2 : z^2,$$

where K is the area of the triangle on y.

By composition of proportion we now obtain

$$K : R : R + S = y^2 : x^2 - y^2 : z^2 - y^2$$

and finally

$$R : S = x^2 - y^2 : z^2 - x^2.$$

Therefore R and S are equal.